Acclaim for Witold Rybczynski and

Waiting for the Weekend

"Gracefully written and insightful . . . An important and entertaining study of the two days that often shape our entire week—and our lives."
— *The Atlanta Journal & Constitution*

"Engaging, informative, and enlightening . . . *Waiting for the Weekend* is filled with rewards. Its style is clear and lucid. Its details are fascinating and wide-ranging. Its author is a very special writer."
— *The Houston Post*

"*Waiting for the Weekend* carries its learning lightly . . . and is infused with a personal voice that is at once charming and intelligent. Those of you who wonder why your weekends aren't fun anymore might consider putting this book on your list of things 'To Do.'"
— *The Boston Globe*

"Wide-ranging and provocative, is a brief but lively addendum to such monumental works in the field as Philippe Aries and Georges Duby's multi-volume *A History of Private Life*."
— *San Francisco Chronicle*

"A companionable ramble along a winding pathway of cultural history in a quiet and thinking book, a kind of intellectual browse that's—well, perfect for a leisurely weekend's reading."
— *Kirkus Reviews*

"A provocative, wonderfully readable essay . . . A subtle lesson in reclaiming the weekend as our own."
— *USA Today*

PENGUIN BOOKS

WAITING FOR THE WEEKEND

Witold Rybczynski's works include *Home* and *The Most Beautiful House in the World*, a national best-seller. Mr. Rybczynski is a professor at McGill University and lives near Montreal with his wife.

Witold Rybczynski

Waiting for the Weekend

PENGUIN BOOKS

PENGUIN BOOKS
Published by the Penguin Group
Viking Penguin, a division of Penguin Books USA Inc.,
375 Hudson Street, New York, New York 10014, U.S.A.
Penguin Books Ltd, 27 Wrights Lane, London W8 5TZ, England
Penguin Books Australia Ltd, Ringwood, Victoria, Australia
Penguin Books Canada Ltd, 10 Alcorn Avenue, Suite 300,
Toronto, Ontario, Canada M4V 3B2
Penguin Books (N.Z.) Ltd, 182–190 Wairau Road,
Auckland 10, New Zealand

Penguin Books Ltd, Registered Offices:
Harmondsworth, Middlesex, England

First published in the United States of America
by Viking Penguin, a division of Penguin Books USA Inc., 1991
Published in Penguin Books 1992

10 9 8 7 6 5 4 3 2 1

THE LIBRARY OF CONGRESS HAS CATALOGUED THE HARDCOVER AS FOLLOWS:
Rybczynski, Witold.
Waiting for the weekend / Witold Rybczynski.
p.   cm.
Includes bibliographical references and index.
ISBN 0-670-83001-1 (hc.)
ISBN 0 14 01.2663 5 (pbk.)
1. Leisure.   2. Recreation.   I. Title.
GV174.R94   1991
790.01'35—dc20   90–50760

Printed in the United States of America
Set in Bembo
Designed by Marysarah Quinn

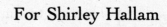
For Shirley Hallam

The days that make us happy make us wise.

—JOHN MASEFIELD

Contents

Waiting for
the Weekend

one

Free Time

Early this morning, before sitting down to write, I listened, once again, to Vivaldi's *The Four Seasons.* I have heard this work so often that the ordered progression of notes holds few surprises, but the melodious singing of the conversing violins still touches me. It is the mystery of music that repeated listenings bring more, not less pleasure.

I am sure I would enjoy the four concertos if they were merely titled Opus 8 (of which they are actually the first part), but like most listeners I am attracted to the images suggested by the lyrical title. My father, who is a musician, disapproves of my admiration for this popular work—I think he considers its conceit maudlin—but I find the descriptive character of the pieces engaging. And, regarding the theme, Vivaldi was explicit, for when the concertos were published, in 1725, he included in the manuscript score the text of four clarifying sonnets—possibly of his own writ-

1

ing—which he keyed to the music by guide letters. The sonnets depicted the changing climate of the four seasons, and portrayed nature as a backdrop for various rural scenes: a goatherd and his barking dog, peasants celebrating the harvest, a huntsman setting out at first light, the comfort of a winter fireside. The score, in turn, represented these scenes, often imitatively: the solo violin taking the part of the lounging goatherd, and the violas his barking dog; the songs of a goldfinch, a turtledove, and a cuckoo were also musically rendered.

Antonio Vivaldi was a native of Venice, where he was choirmaster at a girls' orphanage. Although he was a priest, he composed secular as well as religious music, and his reputation as a violinist and composer (he wrote more than forty operas) spread throughout northern Italy, where he was known as *il Prete Rosso*—the Red Priest—on account of his red hair. Eventually he was acclaimed in all the musical centers of Europe.* It is hardly surprising, then, that when *The Four Seasons* appeared, it achieved immediate and widespread popularity. The work was, to some extent, a towns-

---

* Vivaldi's fame was short-lived, and after his death he and his music were forgotten. It was not until the middle of the nineteenth century that his music began to be listened to anew, and more than a hundred years later before it returned to widespread public favor—there is still no separate entry for Vivaldi in my 1949 edition of the *Encyclopaedia Britannica*.

man's celebration of the pastoral—a celebration that is poignant since the composer was sickly and often housebound—and it fashionably reflected the eighteenth century's artistic preoccupation with the idealization of "Nature." But one did not need to be an artist to appreciate the music; its popularity had a lot to do with the familiarity of its subject.

During the eighteenth century, the change of seasons had a considerable influence on everyday life, and for most of Vivaldi's original audience, *The Four Seasons* vividly described a reality that was immediately recognizable. At different times of year one ate different foods, wore different clothes, indulged in different recreations, performed different agricultural tasks, even inhabited different parts of the house—in Italian country villas, for instance, the rooms on the sunny south side were used in the winter, those on the north side during the hot months. The varying length of the summer and winter day in a city such as Venice affected human behavior. Summers were for sitting on the terrace in front of the Caffè Florian; early winter dusk hurried people indoors. Last, and not least, domestic comfort varied according to the season; the cold, damp winters in poorly heated stone apartments made spring all the more welcome.

The comfort of my own home is largely undisturbed by the time of year—electric lighting, efficient heating, and proper insulation have seen to that.

Since, unlike my neighbors, I am not a farmer, the weather doesn't affect my livelihood. Nevertheless, gardening, storing firewood for the winter, raking leaves, walking the dog, and simply eating breakfast on the porch have made me aware of different times of year in a more acute way than when I lived in a city. A patch of gray cloud, glimpsed between tall buildings as one hurried down the street, could be ignored; in the open country, a looming gray sky can affect the course of my entire day. A storm in town always seemed to be taking place somewhere else; here, thunderclaps batter my house unrelentingly, and the lightning is sometimes so close it smells. That is why, although I have listened to this recording of *The Four Seasons* for more than twenty years, the familiar music has recently found a new resonance in my own life.

.There are probably several reasons for this delayed appreciation. I was brought up in cities and towns, where seasonal variation was less noticeable—at least to me. With the insouciance of childhood, I was indifferent to the elements: playing in the snow until my fingers started turning numb inside the soggy mittens, or splashing about on a cold Maine beach, happy despite shivering skin and chattering teeth. Of course, I remember the various annual activities— summer swimming, winter skiing, helping my father in the garden in the spring, playing football in the fall—but these took place in a vague continuum of changing weather to which, like most children, I gave little thought.

The progression itself of the times of year left little imprint on my consciousness. What I remember more vividly is the rhythmic cadence of the week—days at home and days at school. Probably this rotation has stuck in my mind because I disliked school. My earliest recollection (but it may be only a recollection of what was told me later—an oft-repeated family story) is of being taken for the first time to a London convent school and immediately running away, tearfully rejoining my departing father in the street. A companion memory involves Sundays—not accompanying my parents to church, but being sent to a corner pub for my weekly treat: an exotic imported bottle of Coca-Cola. The texture of the heavy, knurled glass bottle and the smell of the oak casks and beer are with me still.

For most of my boyhood, schooldays retained their coercive character. When I was eleven years old, living in Canada, I was sent to a boarding school in Montreal. We lived close to the city, and I was able to return home each Friday evening. I was attached to my parents, and Sunday afternoons unfailingly brought lachrymose departures. What emotion, what unhappiness! I might have been a cabin boy being sent away on a three-year voyage aboard a clipper ship instead of a grade-schooler going only thirty miles away, and only for five days. But five days was an eternity to someone whose horizon extended only as far as the next Friday evening.

The following year I became a commuter. During the week I rose at six o'clock and bicycled to the train station; in the winter there was a parental carpool. The train journey took about an hour. I liked trains—steam engines still, with real conductors wearing dark-blue uniforms and low-slung leather pouches—and the travel time passed pleasantly enough. There were several of us going to the same school and we sat together, doing homework, reading, and arguing—perfecting our Jesuitical debating skills. I also learned many card games. Still, I looked forward to the end of the week. There was homework to complete, and some household chores (not many, as I recall), but I could sleep late and play with my friends, go on outings in the countryside, or simply stay in my room, reading. For two days, my time was my own.

After my third year of high school I got a summer job on a local weekly newspaper. I worked in the print shop, operating a machine that produced plastic engravings of photographs and illustrations that were then glued to blocks of wood and placed in the form. This did not take all my time, and I also learned to run a terrifying paper-trimming guillotine. Occasionally I was allowed to set the lead slugs that were spewed out of a rattling Linotype. Once a week, the large flatbed cylinder press that stood at the far end of the shop was started up, and we took turns feeding newsprint into the noisy machine. It was not unpleasant work, since the variety of the tasks assigned mitigated the monotony of what were really dull and repetitive operations. Still, when I pushed my time card into the punch-clock on Friday, I savored the satisfying and conclusive clang that signaled two days of freedom.

When I went to college, the personal liberty that I anticipated I would enjoy as a university student—"The best years of your life," adults assured me—was slow to materialize. I was confronted by a rigorous and crowded classroom schedule that left me little free time during the day. Students of architecture were obliged to take two years of engineering, and I struggled with chemistry, physics, and calculus, subjects for which my classical education had left me unprepared and which consequently engaged me not at all. Nor did it help that the classes were large and anonymous; mine was simply one more unformed face in a crowd of more or less interested freshmen (and in engineering they *were* mostly men), dutifully scribbling notes on their clipboards.

Of course, it wasn't all work. I joined a rifle club, but the initial attraction—I had never owned a gun— wore off quickly, and I soon tired of the noisy and dark firing range. I became a member of a drama group and happily worked first as a stage manager and later as a set designer. What free time I had was now spent either hanging around the basement office of the Players Club, in rehearsals, or caught up in the excitement of producing plays. The theater not only got me out of the intellectual wasteland of the faculty of engineering and introduced me to Fernando Arrabal and Dylan Thomas, it also brought me into the company of actors, and so allowed me to meet girls.

What with commuting, and attending a boy's school, my experience of the opposite sex was scant, which made my induction into that important university institution—Saturday Night—all the more memorable. I had to learn the unwritten protocols of dating that, during the early 1960s, represented society's vain attempt to control adolescent libidos. There were forms to be observed: the anxious weekday phone call, the formalities of dress, the proprieties of hand-holding, and the delicate progression of necking.

The chief convention of the date was the pretext of going out—usually to a party or to a movie. I developed a taste for jazz, and spent my weekend nights at clubs and bars, listening to visiting American stars: Bill Evans, Charles Mingus, Thelonious Monk, and the great drummer Max Roach. My interest in the last was partly occupational, for I, too, played drums. Since my two roommates were musicians, we played together on weekends, sometimes at jam sessions, occasionally for pay. Two days a week I was a nocturnal hipster. It was the early sixties, and although we grew beards and wore sunglasses—shades—we did not consider ourselves Beats; like the musicians whom we admired, we dressed in conservative three-piece suits and drank Scotch on the rocks. We took our music more seriously than our studies.

My double life ended when I left the university and got a job—as an architect's assistant, not a drummer, for by then my performing career had faltered. But working in an office, as I already knew from my summer experiences, meant that the familiar five-and-two rhythm persisted, reinforced now by the contractual obligation I had to my employer. I enjoyed my job, and often looked archly down on the crowd of office workers that streamed out of our building punctually at five o'clock at the end of each day. My co-workers and I often kept longer hours, meeting the frequent deadlines that characterize architectural practice; still, were we so different? We would have hated to admit it, but we, too, looked forward to the end of the week.

A historical shift has occurred in timekeeping between Vivaldi's time, and my own—a shift from the pastoral to the industrial, from the natural to the artificial. I could not describe my life in four concertos but in recurring variations—the Weekend Variations: carefree and playful schoolboy weekends at home; college weekends, livelier now, not just jazz but the sweet fumbling of adolescent infatuation; a young man's nighttime weekends, full of drink, talk, and alternating loneliness and romance.

Because my free time was personally enjoyed, I imagined that it was personally regulated, but this was not quite so. True, I did what I thought I wanted, but certainly not *when* I wanted; I dutifully arranged my recreations to fall in step with the regularly scheduled weekly intermissions that were accorded me. Not that I felt this was an imposition. It was done so automatically, it seemed so normal, that I never gave the presence of the weekend a second thought—it was simply the way life was.

That was twenty years ago. The sovereignty of the weekend has, if anything, grown in the interval, and it now conditions our behavior to an even greater degree. On Monday mornings we recount our weekend adventures and commiserate with one another as we begin a week of labor. By Tuesday, the weekend is slipping into memory. Wednesday is called "Midweek" in German, and it is exactly that—a hiatus. On Thursday we begin to anticipate the weekend. We listen uneasily to the divinations of the weatherman—will there be snow for skiing, or good weather for the beach?—as we anxiously make preparations for the weekend. "Thank God It's Friday"—a phrase of the sixties—flags the end of the week, or rather the beginning of the weekend. Another signal of the weekend, at least in California, is "Jeans Friday," when many offices suspend their normal dress codes and let their employees dress as they please; in Hawaii, "Aloha Friday" is observed by wearing colorful print shirts.

The word "weekend," which started life as the grammatically correct "week-end," lost its hyphen somewhere along the way, ceasing to be merely the end of the week and acquiring, instead, an autonomous and sovereign existence. "Have a good weekend," we say to each other, never "Have a good week." Where once the week consisted of weekdays and Sunday, it now comprises weekdays and the weekend. Ask most people to name the first day of the week and they will answer "Monday, of course"; fifty years ago the answer would have been Sunday. Wall calendars still show Sunday as the first day of the week, and children are taught the days of the week starting with Sunday, but how long will these conventions last? Sunday, once the day of rest, has become merely one of two days of what is often strenuous activity. Although we continue to celebrate the traditional religious and civic holidays—holy days—these now account for only a small portion of our total nonworking days, and are overshadowed by the 104 days of secular weekends—more, if you count long weekends.

The long weekend probably began accidentally, when a public holiday occurring on a Friday or a Monday happily added a day to the weekend. One of the first predictable long weekends in Canada and the United States occurred when the first Monday in September—Labor Day—was declared a legal holiday. Columbus Day, and lately Martin Luther King Day, followed suit; so did Thanksgiving in Canada. The American Thanksgiving was set on a Thursday, which for many means a four-day weekend. In the case of traditional national holidays that do not fall on a Monday, such as Independence Day or Canada Day, although official celebrations are held on the appointed date, it is not uncommon for employers to shift the actual day off to make it an appendage to the weekend.

These sanctioned long weekends seem to have whetted our appetite, with the result that additional do-it-yourself long weekends have proliferated. Surprisingly, they have done so at the expense of the traditional vacation. Many families choose to dispense with—or reduce—their two- or three-week holidays, and instead attach a sprinkling of days to weekends throughout the year. The weekend has also expanded in another way, as early-Friday-afternoon office closings have become commonplace, at least during the

summer. The pushy weekend seems destined to nib-
ble away at the week.

This new time structure is important, for it affects
not only *when* we relax but also *how* we relax. For
most of us, life assumes a different rhythm on the
weekend; we sleep in, cut the grass, wash the car. We
also go to the movies, especially during hot weather.
(The sixteen weekends between mid-May and Labor
Day are when Hollywood studios traditionally launch
their summer blockbusters—in 1990 there were fifty
movies jostling each other for box-office primacy.)
But the weekend is not merely an occasion for lazing
about. There are weekend sales to go to, weekend
rates to take advantage of, weekend discount tickets
to buy, weekend clothes to wear. And weekend bags
to pack for weekend invitations, for the weekend
means not only shopping and recreation, it also means
travel. The travel may be distant, but more likely it
takes the city dweller to the countryside on the outskirts of the city, to the cottage and the ski chalet.
There are entire towns and villages whose economic
life is centered on this weekend migration, and many
industries that rely on business generated by the two-
day break, such as do-it-yourself home-repair centers,
boatbuilders, and sports equipment manufacturers.

The weekend is a time for physical exercise and
games. Some of these pastimes, like tennis, have a
long history and a newfound popularity; others,

like whitewater canoeing, windsurfing, or hang gliding, are more recent. Most are distinguished from nineteenth-century recreations such as croquet and golf by their relative arduousness and even riskiness. These periodic bursts of physical activity have their own consequences, however, and sports-medicine clinics report a growing number of Monday-morning injuries as weekend athletes recover from strained tennis elbows, jogging knees, and twisted skiing ankles. Scraped elbows and peeling, sunburned noses are as much a weekend institution as the lakeside cottage, the yard sale, and the Sunday brunch.

And, of course, the Sunday paper. The first Sunday paper was the London *Observer,* which started in 1791, and soon had many competitors. The first American Sunday paper was published in Baltimore, in 1796, but it folded after one issue—the religious tradition against selling papers on Sunday proved too strong. In the post–Civil War era, attitudes changed and Sunday editions of dailies appeared; by 1900 there were 639 of them. The Sunday paper owes its present form to Joseph Pulitzer, whose gaudy *Sunday World* pioneered colored comics and the color supplement, and included book reviews, exotic travel articles, dime novels, women's pages, a youth department, and a science column—something for everyone in the family. The *Sunday World* was a great success (department-store advertising made it a money-maker) and circulation was huge, more than five times that

14

of the daily edition, for Pulitzer realized that on Sunday readers wanted something different. The weekdays were for news; Sunday was for leisure.

The chief Oxford English Dictionary definition of leisure is "Time which one can spend as one pleases." That is, "free" time. But in one of his popular columns in the *Illustrated London News*—a Sunday paper—G. K. Chesterton pointed out that leisure should not be confused with liberty. Contrary to most people's expectations, the presence of the first by no means assured the availability of the second. This confusion arose, according to Chesterton, because the term "leisure" was used to describe three different things: "The first is being allowed to do something. The second is being allowed to do anything. And the third (and perhaps most rare and precious) is being allowed to do nothing." The first, he acknowledged, was the most common form of leisure, and the one which of late—he was writing in the early 1900s— had shown the greatest quantitative increase. The second—the liberty to fashion what one willed out of one's leisure time—was more restricted, and tended to be confined to artists and other creative individuals. It was the third, however, that was obviously his favorite since it allowed idleness—which was, in Chesterton's view, the truest form of leisure.

Perhaps only someone as portly as Chesterton— Maisie Ward, his biographer, estimated he weighed almost three hundred pounds—could rhapsodize over

15

idleness. More likely, inactivity attracted him because he was the least lazy of men; his bibliography lists more than one hundred published books—essays, poetry, biographies, novels, and short stories. He was also a magazine editor, and a popular lecturer and broadcaster. Although he managed to cram this all into a relatively short life—he died at sixty-two—as his physique would suggest, it was a life replete with material enjoyments, and surprisingly unhurried. Not a life of leisure, perhaps, but carried out at a leisurely pace.

Chesterton's observation—that modern society provided many opportunities for leisure but made it "more and more easy to get some things and impossible to get others"—continues to be true. Should you want to play tennis or golf, for example, courts and courses abound. Fancy a video? There are plenty of specialty stores, lending libraries, and mail-order clubs. Lepidopterists, on the other hand, have a difficult time finding unfenced countryside in which to practice their avocation. If your pastime is laying bricks, and you do not have a rural estate—as Winston Churchill had—you will not find a bricklaying franchise at your neighborhood mall.* Better take up golf instead.

---

* Churchill was a skillful and prolific bricklayer. At Chartwell, he built two cottages, a play house, and several walls. In one letter he wrote: "I have had a delightful month building a cottage and dictating a book: 200 bricks and 2,000 words a day."

Chesterton argued that a man compelled by lack of choice—or by social pressure—to play golf in the afternoon, when he would rather be attending to some solitary hobby, was not so different from the slave who might have several hours of leisure while his overseer slept but who had to be ready to work at a moment's notice. Neither could be said to be the master of his leisure. They had free time, but not freedom. To press this parallel further, have we become enslaved by the weekend?

At first glance, it is an odd question, for surely it is our work that enslaves us, not our recreations. We call people who become obsessed by their jobs workaholics, but we don't have a word for someone who is possessed by play. Maybe we should. I have many acquaintances for whom weekend activities seem more important than workaday existence, and who behave as if the week were merely an irritating interference in their real, extracurricular lives. I sometimes have the impression that to really know these weekend sailors, mountain climbers, or horsewomen, I would have to accompany them on their outings and excursions—see them in their natural habitat, so to speak. But would I see a different person, or merely the same one governed by different conventions of comportment, behavior, accoutrement, and dress?

I'm always charmed by old photographs of skiers that show groups of people in what appear to be street clothes, with uncomplicated pieces of bent wood strapped to sturdy walking boots. These men and women have a playful and unaffected air. Today every novice is caparisoned in skintight spandex like an Olympic racer, and even cross-country skiing, a simple enough pastime, has been infected by a preoccupation with correct dress, authentic terminology, and up-to-date equipment. This reflects a concern for status and consumption, but it also suggests an attitude to play that is different from what it was in the past. Most outdoor sports, once simply muddled through, are now undertaken with a high degree of seriousness. "Professional" used to be a word that distinguished someone who was paid for performing an activity from the sportsman; today the word has increasingly come to denote anyone with a high degree of proficiency; "professional-quality" equipment is available to—and desired by—all. Conversely, "amateur," a wonderful word literally meaning "lover," has been degraded to mean a rank beginner, or anyone without a certain level of skill. "Just an amateur," we say; it is not, as it once was, a compliment.

The lack of carelessness in our recreation, the sense of obligation to get things right, and the emphasis on protocol and decorum do represent an enslavement of a kind. People used to "play" tennis; now they "work" on their backhand. It is not hard to imagine what Chesterton would have thought of such dedication; this was just the sort of laborious pursuit of play that he so often derided. "If a thing is worth doing at all," he once wrote, "it is worth doing badly."

Chesterton held the traditional view that leisure was different from the type of recreation typically afforded by the modern weekend. His own leisure pastimes included an eclectic mix of the unfashionable and the bohemian—sketching, collecting weapons, and playing with the cardboard cutouts of his toy theater. Leisure was the opportunity for personal, even idiosyncratic pursuits, not for ordered recreation, for private reverie rather than for public spectacles. If a sport was undertaken, it was for the love of playing, not of winning, not even of playing well. Above all, free time was to remain that: free of the encumbrance of convention, free of the need for busyness, free for the "noble habit of doing nothing." That hardly describes the modern weekend.

What is the meaning of the weekday-weekend cycle? Is it yet another symptom of the standardization and bureaucratization of everyday life that social critics such as Lewis Mumford or Jacques Ellul have warned about? Is the weekend merely the cunning marketing ploy of a materialist culture, a device to increase consumption? Is it a deceptive placebo to counteract the boredom and meaninglessness of the workplace?

Or is this the heralded Leisure Society? If so, it is hardly what was anticipated. The decades leading up to the 1930s saw a continuing reduction in the number of hours in the workweek—from sixty to fifty to thirty-five. There was every reason to think that this trend would continue and workdays would grow shorter and shorter. This, and massive automation, would lead to what was then starting to be referred to as "universal leisure." Not everyone agreed that this would be a good thing; there was much speculation about what people would do with their newfound freedom, and some psychologists worried that universal leisure would really mean universal boredom. Hardly, argued the optimists; it would provide opportunities for self-improvement, adult education, and a blossoming of the creative arts. Others were less sanguine about the prospects for creative ease in a society that had effectively glorified labor, and argued that Americans lacked the sophistication and inner resources to deal with a life without work.

Universal leisure did not come to pass, or at least it did not arrive in the expected form. For one thing, the workday appears to have stabilized at about eight hours. Automation has reduced jobs in certain industries, as was predicted, but overall employment has increased, not decreased, although not necessarily in high-paying jobs. Women have entered the workforce, with the result that more, not less, people are working; since housework still needs to be done, it could be argued that, in many families, there is really less leisure than before.

There may not be more leisure, but there is no doubt that the development of the weekend has caused a redistribution of leisure time, which for many people has effectively shortened the length of the workweek. This redistribution—coupled with more disposable income—has made it possible to undertake recreation in a variety of unexpected ways—some creative, some not—and not only at annual intervals, on vacations, but throughout the year, every weekend.

All this has called into question the traditional relationship between leisure and work, a relationship about which our culture has always been ambivalent. Generally speaking, there are two opposing schools of thought. On the one hand there is the ideal, held by thinkers as disparate as Karl Marx and the Catholic philosopher Josef Pieper, of a society increasingly emancipated from labor. This notion echoes the Aristotelian view that the goal of life is happiness, and that leisure, as distinguished from amusement and recreation, is the state necessary for its achievement. "It is commonly believed that happiness depends on leisure," Aristotle wrote in his *Ethics,* "because we occupy ourselves so that we may have leisure, just as we make war in order that we may live at peace." Or, to put it more succinctly, as did the title of

Lover Boy's 1982 hit song, we are "Working for the Weekend."

Opposed to this is the more modern (so-called Protestant) work ethic that values labor for its own sake, and sees its reduction—or, worse, its elimination—as an unthinkable degradation of human life. "There is no substitute for work except other serious work," wrote Lewis Mumford, who considered that meaningful work was the highest form of human activity and who once went so far as to liken the abolition of work to a malignant Final Solution. According to this view, work should be its own reward, whether it is factory work, housework, or a workout. Leisure, equated with idleness, is suspect; leisure without toil, or disconnected from it, is altogether sinister. The weekend is not free time but break time—an intermission.

But I am getting ahead of myself. I want first to examine something that will shed light on the relation between work and leisure: how we came to adopt a rigorous division of our everyday lives into five days of work and two of play, and how the weekend became the chief temporal institution of the modern age. And how, in turn, this universally accepted structure has affected the course and nature of our leisure— whether it involves playing golf, laying bricks, or just daydreaming.

two

Week After Week

Listening to music, lying on the beach, being caught up in some pleasurable activity, we sometimes feel that we have lost track of time. "Time flies when you're having fun," we say, underlining the carefree and spontaneous character of play. It is ironic, then, that our chief occasion for leisure—the weekend—is the direct product of the mechanical practice of measuring time.

Counting days in chunks of seven now comes so naturally that it's easy to forget this is an unusual way to mark the passage of time. Day spans the interval between the rising and setting of the sun; the twenty-four-hour day is the duration between one dawn and the next. The month measures—or once did—the time required for the moon to wax, become full, and wane; and the year counts one full cycle of the seasons. What does the week measure? Nothing. At least, nothing visible. No natural phenomenon occurs every seven days—nothing happens to the sun, the moon, or the stars. The week is an artificial, man-made interval.

Generally speaking, our calendar is a flexible affair, full of inconsistencies. The length of the day varies with the season; the duration of the month is likewise irregular. Adjustments need to be made: every four years we add a day to February; every four hundred years we add a day to the centurial year. The week, on the other hand, is exactly seven days long, now and forever. We say that there are fifty-two weeks in a year, but that is an approximation, since the week is not a subdivision of either the month or the year. The week mocks the calendar and marches relentlessly and unbroken across time, paying no attention to the seasons. The British scholar F. H. Colson—who in 1926 wrote a fascinating monograph on the subject—described the week as an "intruder." It was an intruder who arrived relatively late. The week was made the final feature of what became the definitive Western calendar sometime in the second or third century A.D., in ancient Rome. But it can be glimpsed in different guises—not always seven days long, and not always continuous—in many earlier civilizations.

The oldest calendar is that of the Egyptians; if one includes the Copts, Parsis, and Iranians, who all adopted variations of the Egyptian calendar, it has been in use for five thousand years. The Egyptians divided the year into three seasons—inundation, seed-

time, and harvest—which reflected the annual prog-
ress of their Nilotic, agricultural society. They also
divided the year into months, first ten and later
twelve. Day and night had twelve hours each. Daytime hours were counted by means of shadowclocks;
at night the hours were reckoned according to the
movement of thirty-six different stars. The particular
stars used for timekeeping changed every ten days,
and as a result the thirty-day Egyptian civil month
was sectioned into three ten-day periods called decades, which roughly corresponded to the waxing,
middle, and waning of the moon. It is tempting to
describe these ten-day intervals as "weeks"; unfor-
tunately there is little evidence about their civic or
religious functions, and they may have been only an
astronomical convenience.

The Mesopotamian calendars of Sumer, Babylon,
and Assyria likewise divided the year into twelve
months. Each month of twenty-nine days was further
divided in two by a special day—*shabattu*—which
commemorated the full moon. This produced a time-
interval of fourteen days. By the seventh century B.C.,
the seventh, twenty-first, and twenty-eighth days of
the month were also assigned special importance, and
on these days many common work activities were
proscribed.

This septenary scheme has led some scholars to
refer to the interim periods as "lunar weeks." In fact,

the Mesopotamian month varied from twenty-nine to thirty days, and each of the four seven-day periods was followed by a one- or two-day break, which made the seven-day periods, unlike the true week, discontinuous. Nevertheless, the idea of a relatively short period of time followed regularly by a day or two devoted to leisure, is strikingly similar.

Like the Egyptians, the Athenians divided the month into three periods of about ten days each. The first was called "the waxing moon," the last "the waning moon," and the middle period was unnamed. The days within each decade were numbered, as in "the second day of the waxing moon" or, "the fourth day of the middle period." The days of the third decade were counted backward, however, which indicated how many were left until the end of the month, customarily the time for settling debts and paying bills. Unlike the week, however, the decade did not measure the interval between civic holidays, which were set according to a different calendar.

The republican Roman calendar designated three special dividing days in each thirty- or thirty-one-day month. The first of the month was called the Calends, the fifth (or seventh in one of the four long months) the Nones, and the thirteenth (or fifteenth) the Ides. The three "marker days" were special days for important public events, when religious ceremonies were carried out and certain activities proscribed. Although the intervals were of markedly differing duration—three days, seven days, sixteen days (in a short month)—they performed a function similar to that of the week.

Two other well-known ancient calendars are those of the Chinese and Mayan civilizations. The Chinese calendar included a cycle of individually named days, which resembled the week in its recurring progression throughout the year but which was much longer— sixty days instead of seven. The Mayan civil calendar included a succession of thirteen-day periods, numbered to indicate the thirteen gods of the Mayan upper world. These periods were repeated twenty times— the Mayas were obsessed by the number twenty and used a vigesimal mathematical system—to complete a full cycle. This thirteen-day period—a kind of week—seems to have had no civil function, and was used primarily for religious and ceremonial purposes.

The common feature of ancient calendar-making was a recognition of the waxing and waning of the moon. It took no sophisticated instruments to observe the moon; nor was a knowledge of mathematics or astronomy required to note that the phases of the moon, from the arrival of the new moon to the disappearance of the old, were regular. The origin of the Roman marker days, for example, is considered to have been lunar, for they would have fallen on the first sighting of the new moon, the first quarter, and the full moon. The twenty-nine- and thirty-day lunar months—"mooneths"—became the basis for the so-called lunar year used by the Babylonians. The lunar month continues to control both the Jewish and the Islamic calendars, as well as the allocation of Hindu festivals.

The lunar cycle was memorable because it was relatively short—it takes about twenty-nine and a half days for the moon to make its circuit—and so it was more practical as a timekeeper than the annual movement of the sun or the change of seasons. There was a problem with the 354-day lunar year, however. It takes the earth about 365 days to perform one revolution in its orbit around the sun, or, to put it another way, it takes about 365 days (a solar year) to complete a cycle of the four seasons. This means that there is roughly an eleven-day discrepancy between the lunar and the solar years. Hence a calendar based on the phases of the moon slowly retrogressed through the year, relative to the seasons, repeating only every thirty-two and a half years. The practical implication of this fluidity was a lack of concordance between the month and the time of year—sometimes December occurred in the winter, sometimes in the summer. To keep the lunar months in step with the seasons, it was necessary to add several days at the end of each year, which is what the Egyptians, Greeks, and Romans all did.

It was Julius Caesar who, with the aid of the Greek astronomer, Sosigenes, totally reformed the Roman calendar, in 46 B.C. The Julian calendar was based on the solar year, and although it kept the traditional names of the twelve months, which we still use, these were no longer lunar months, but varied in length so that they added up to 365 days. Since the solar year is really six hours longer than 365 days, an extra day was added every fourth year, the leap year. A slight imprecision was rectified by Pope Gregory in the six-teenth century, otherwise the Julian calendar has proved remarkably durable.*

Strikingly absent in the Julian calendar was any-thing resembling the week. Since the Julian months varied—twenty-eight, thirty, and thirty-one days—they could not be neatly subdivided into decades (as could the thirty-day Egyptian civic month). And yet, within two hundred years or so, almost all Roman citizens were familiar with the seven-day week. How did this happen?

To begin with, there were many "sevens" in the ancient world: the Seven Names of God, the Seven Pillars of Wisdom, the Seven Labors of Hercules, the Seven Sleepers of Ephesus, the Seven Against Thebes,

---

* The Gregorian calendar was adopted first by Roman Catholic countries in 1582, and eventually spread to Protestant northern Europe; Britain, insular as ever, held out until 1752. It was adopted in Japan in 1873, in China in 1912, and in Russia as late as 1918.

the Seven Sages of Greece, and the Seven Wonders of the World. There was a cycle of Roman stories called the Seven Wise Masters that also occurred in Greek, Arabic, and Sanskrit. And, of course, the imperial city was built on seven hills.

Seven appeared as a magical number first among the Babylonians, as early as the third millennium B.C., and played an important role in their calendar.* One of the roots of this septenary fascination was mathematical; seven is a prime number. Another was astronomical. There were seven heavenly bodies with apparent motion in the night sky—the "erring seven," the "seven wanderers," that is, the planets. These were Saturn, Jupiter, Mars, the Sun, Mercury, Venus, and the Moon (which the ancients considered a planet), to give them in the usual order of their decreasing distance from the earth. Whether the seven planets of antiquity suggested the belief in the magic number or merely reinforced it is not clear. In any case, as astronomy—and astrology—spread from Babylon to Greece, Egypt, and Rome, the seven heavenly bodies became identified with the great gods of the pantheon.

---

* The cult of the magical number seven has been found in virtually every part of the world, including India and China. In some places, such as Africa and the Pacific, it has been attributed to Islamic or European influences; its presence among many American Indian tribes is more difficult to explain.

Astrology maintained that the movements of the planets represented the activities of the gods themselves, and that every earthly occurrence was influenced by the position of the stars and other heavenly bodies. Individual planets were identified with metals, colors, and animals. The sun, for example, was associated with gold, the color yellow, the cock (which crowed at dawn), the lion (which was tawny), and with certain spices such as cloves and cinnamon. Each of the seven ages of man (infancy, childhood, adolescence, youth, manhood, early old age, old age) was governed by one of the planets. Not surprisingly, each day was likewise under the influence of a different planetary god, and since there were seven planets, this produced a cycle of seven days. Or so we assume, for there is no surviving information regarding the earliest manifestation of what became known as the planetary week.

The actual order of the days in the planetary week did not follow the usual order of the planets, however. The first hour of the first day was assigned to Saturn, who thus ruled that day; the second hour to Jupiter, the third to Mars, and so on. The eighth hour started the series all over again. Following this progression, the twenty-fifth hour, that is, the first hour of the second day, turned out to belong to the Sun, which thus ruled that day. This produced a planetary week as follows:

Dies Saturni (Saturn)
Dies Solis (Sun)
Dies Lunae (Moon)
Dies Martis (Mars)
Dies Mercurii (Mercury)
Dies Iovis (Jupiter)
Dies Veneris (Venus)

Of course, the Jews already kept a seven-day week, organized around the observance of the Sabbath. It is possible—although disputed by many scholars—that the Jews adapted this method of timekeeping from the Babylonians during their exile in that country in the sixth century B.C., and converted the Babylonian *shabattu* into their Sabbath, a day of religious observance when all work was proscribed. Or they may simply have been influenced by the Babylonian belief in the magical number seven. Either way, the correspondence between the Babylonian practice of dividing the lunar month every seven days and the Jewish observance of the Sabbath on every seventh day is surely not coincidental.

There is evidence that by the time of the restoration of Judah, in 140 B.C., the celebration of the Sabbath was a well-established institution. The adoption of a successive seven-day cycle was unusual, and exactly why the Jews evolved this mechanism is unclear. According to the Old Testament, the Sabbath

was "their" day, given to them—and them alone—
by Jehovah. Unquestionably, its very singularity appealed to the exiled Jews as a way of differentiating
themselves from the alien Babylonian Gentiles who
surrounded them. The fact that the Sabbath occurred
on every seventh day, irrespective of the seasons, was
a powerful idea, for it overrode all other existing
calendars.

Religious sects often adopt a temporal distinction
to solidify their fragile identities and to detach themselves from other faiths. The early Christians, for example, deliberately chose a day other than the Sabbath
as the holy day of their week. So did Muhammad,
who designated Friday as the Islamic holy day; indeed,
Saturday and Sunday are regarded as unfortunate days
by Muslims. So did the Adventists who, after the
second coming of Christ failed to occur on October
22, 1844, as they had foretold, decided to observe
Saturday instead of Sunday as the holy day of the
week. The Quakers emphasized their distinctiveness
by replacing the planetary names of the days with
numbers: First Day, Second Day, and so on.

The exclusiveness of the Jewish faith precluded the
widespread adoption of the Sabbath by others, and
for centuries the seven-day week remained a uniquely
Jewish institution. Or almost so. The Jews were a
small but influential minority in the Roman Empire,
and their observance of the Sabbath did not go un-

noticed by the superstitious Romans. There is some evidence that both Greeks and Romans came to associate the Jewish holiday with Saturn, the unlucky planet, which confirmed it (in their eyes) as a day on which it was prudent to do as little as possible. In any case, in towns where there were large numbers of Jewish traders and shopkeepers, it was convenient for everyone to observe the same holiday.

Historians have been unable to fully unravel the relationship between the planetary week and the Jewish week. The Jewish week is obviously connected to the planetary week, but how? In the planetary week each day is devoted to a different deity and is considered important; for the Jews, the week in itself was merely the interval between the Sabbaths. They called Sunday, Monday, and Tuesday the days "after the Sabbath," and Wednesday, Thursday, and Friday the days "before"; in the modern Jewish calendar the weekdays are assigned numbers (first, second, third, and so on), not names. If the Sabbath did not inspire the planetary week, perhaps it was the other way around? There is a theory that the Jews rearranged the planetary week to start on the Sun's Day—instead of Saturn's—after the Exodus, as an expression of their hatred for their Egyptian oppressors, and when they adopted the Sabbath (the seventh day) it fell on Saturn's Day.

The origin of the planetary week is likewise obscure, as regards both place and time. Dio Cassius, a Roman historian who lived in the third century A.D., thought that the planetary week was conceived in Egypt, but modern scholars dispute this claim; more likely it was a Hellenistic practice that migrated to Rome. Dio Cassius maintained that the planetary week had been a relatively recent invention. There is some evidence, however, of a planetary week during the Augustan period—two hundred years before— and it may have originated even earlier, although probably not much earlier. What is certain is that not long before the time of Dio Cassius, the habit of measuring time in cycles of seven days was already commonplace in private life throughout the Roman Empire.

More curious than the origin of the seven-day week is the question of how it spread. In a relatively short period of time, the "intruder" insinuated itself into the Julian calendar and became common in most of Europe. One would imagine an imperial edict as the starting point. Or, as had been the case with astronomical time-reckoning, one might expect the week to have been the subject of scholarly study and debate. But there is no evidence pointing to either of these. As F. H. Colson pointed out, "There is a complete silence as to any official endorsement or even recognition of the planetary week, and this is a matter in which silence does imply non-existence."

The planetary week did not coincide with any formal rite or celebration, at least not for most Roman citizens. There were some exceptions, but they were not numerous. The early Christians, who adopted the Jewish custom of gathering once every seven days, chose the day after the Sabbath, probably to commemorate the Resurrection of Christ, which was supposed to have occurred on that day. This corresponded to the Sun's Day of the planetary week. That day was also celebrated by another religion—Mithraism. This Persian creed had been brought to Rome in the first century A.D.; it grew in popularity, especially among common people, and eventually received imperial endorsement from Constantine. The magical number seven was important to the Mithraists, so it was not surprising that they, too, celebrated every seventh day; since Mithras, like the sun, was the god of light, they naturally identified with his day of the planetary week.

One should not make too much of the presence of these religious groups in the Roman Empire while the planetary week was spreading. The Jews, for example, were not objects of universal admiration. Nor were the Christians. The Christian church did play a role in the spread of the seven-day week and the observance of Sunday, but that happened much later; in the second century A.D.—when the planetary week was adopted, the Christians were a tiny, persecuted minority. A slightly stronger case can be made for Mithraism. It was particularly popular among soldiers, and this may have assisted the spread of the planetary week in the Empire. It is equally possible, however, that Mithraists simply adapted themselves to an already popular custom. It is unlikely that the influence of *any* of these minority religions would have been powerful enough to explain the widespread adoption of the week.

Judging from the absence of any written record, the week appears to have been spread by word of mouth and adopted by common people. They left no written account, and we can only guess about their motivations. Ordinary people had no exact knowledge of astrology; nevertheless, as Colson suggests, their belief in the influence of the planets must have been profound. The planetary week, in which days were under the sway of compassionate and malevolent deities, may have developed as a kind of superstition, like the belief in the misfortune that is attached to black cats or to the number thirteen. That the week has superstitious overtones is evident in the old nursery rhyme:

> Monday's child is fair of face,
> Tuesday's child is full of grace,

Wednesday's child is full of woe,
Thursday's child has far to go,
Friday's child is loving and giving,
Saturday's child has to work for a living,
But a child that's born on the Sabbath day
Is fair and wise and good and gay.

Monday's child reflects the beauty of the moon; Friday's loving child is under the influence of Venus, the goddess of love; and Saturday's unlucky child falls under the influence of Saturn, the dimmest and slowest of the planets.

Typically, superstitions exhibit an appealing logic—or, more often, an equally appealing lack of it. It makes sense to avoid walking under ladders, but why avoid cracks in the sidewalk? Black cats do look ominous; on the other hand, so do crows. A horseshoe on the wall should be U-shaped to catch luck—if it is mounted upside down, the luck pours out. That *sounds* reasonable, but why a horseshoe, rather than some other found object? Thirteen is ill-starred, eleven is not; salt, not sugar, is thrown over the shoulder, and the left shoulder, not the right. It is possible to discover the original sources of some such practices, but such knowledge is extraneous to the belief itself—the core of superstition is acceptance, not understanding.

I would speculate that the planetary week met with

the same sort of easy acceptance. The people who embraced the week did not ponder why it was seven and not eight days, or why it should be named after the planets rather than some other group of deities, or a different set of astrological star signs. Superstitions emerge out of daily practice, not scholarly inquiry. They are learned at a grandfather's knee, or with one's playmates, not in school. And the fact that they evolve out of a general consensus, rather than being imposed, makes them all the more enduring.

Unlike most superstitions, though, the planetary week was not something that grew out of a local tradition—it was a novelty to the people who so quickly adopted it. But as we have seen, the idea of clustering days into bunches, which generally varied from five to ten—what Daniel Boorstin so charmingly calls bouquets of days—was not unprecedented. The decade attests to the need for a shorter time interval than the lunar month. The observance of regular nonworking days was also common in many societies. This coincided, in most cases, with a practical desire for a shorter regular intermission, whether for religious or social reasons.

There is no historical evidence that the planetary week first used in Greece and Rome began or ended with a holiday. But such a pattern is visible in another part of the world where the planetary week became a popular institution. The planetary week arrived on

the Indian subcontinent early in the fourth century
A.D.; it appears to have been borrowed from Hellenistic sources. The week did not arrive as an integral
part of an imported time-reckoning system. The
Hindu calendars (like the Greeks, they had several)
were—and are—a complicated mixture of Hellenistic,
Babylonian, and Chinese influences, as well as indigenous practices. At some point, Hindus began to observe the first day of the week, *Adivara,* as a day on
which it was considered unlucky to start new en-
deavors. It was therefore a holiday and a market day.
The Sanskrit *Adivara,* like the names of the other days,
corresponded to one of the planetary gods, in this case
the god whom Hindus worshiped every morning—
the god of the sun. It is a curious coincidence that
Hindus should have chosen Sunday as a day of rest,
long before contact with Christian missionaries or
British colonizers.

At about the same time as the week arrived in
India, the Emperor Constantine officially proclaimed
the planetary week and designated the Sun's Day as
a special holiday and as the first day of the week,
altering the earlier tradition that began the planetary
week with Saturn's Day. There were later attempts
to divest the week of its pagan planetary origins by
substituting numbers for planetary day names, and
numbered days still survive in the Portuguese, Greek,
and Slavic languages. On the other hand, the Italians,

French, and Spanish stubbornly maintained the original Roman names for the days of the week—except for Saturday, which was called the Sabbath. The English, German, and Dutch kept the planetary names, but they substituted some of their own analogous deities for the Roman gods. For Mars, Mercury, Jupiter, and Venus they used the Teutonic gods Tiw (or Din), Woden, Thor, and Fria. These differences between the Romance languages and those of northern Europe are illustrated below:

Latin	Italian	French	English	Dutch
Dies Solis	domenica	dimanche	Sunday	Zondag
Dies Lunae	lunedì	lundi	Monday	Maandag
Dies Martis	martedì	mardi	Tuesday	Dinsdag
Dies Mercurii	mercoledì	mercredi	Wednesday	Woensdag
Dies Iovis	giovedì	jeudi	Thursday	Dondersdag
Dies Veneris	venerdì	vendredi	Friday	Vrejdag
Dies Saturni	sabato	samedi	Saturday	Zaterdag

There are different names even for the Christian Sabbath. In English, Dutch, German, and the Scandinavian languages, it has remained the planetary Sunday. Italian, French, Spanish, Portuguese, and Gaelic all use variations of the Latin *dominica* (the Lord's Day); so does modern Greek, although the term is translated. In Russian, Czech, and Polish, on the other hand, Sunday follows neither convention, and is called "not-working day."

There is only one European language that exhibits

a complete and consistent set of Roman planetary names—Welsh. All the rest have incorporated mixtures of planetary names (sometimes derived directly from the Latin root, and sometimes not), religious references, numbers, and a few secular descriptions. Germans, for example, used the Teutonic deities for the names of the week, except for Wednesday, which is "midweek" instead of Wodin's Day, and Saturday, which is the "eve of Sunday." In the Scandinavian languages, which otherwise resemble English, Saturday is not Saturn's Day but "washing day." In Gaelic some days are planetary, but Friday is called "the great fast." Even when days are numbered, there are inconsistencies. In Polish and Russian, since Monday is the "first day," Sunday comes at the end of the week, as in the Judaic calendar. In Portuguese, which also uses numbers instead of names, Monday is called the "second day," as it is in modern Greek. This variety demonstrates that while the adoption of the planetary seven-day week may have been universal, the *meanings* attached to the days of the week were not consistently planetary. In fact, the root of the English word "week" (wicu, wike, wyke, wek, wok) is ancient and predates the planetary week.

This multiplicity of meanings is another explanation for the week's popularity: it was many things to many people, sometimes many things to the same people. It was magical and practical both. A superstition at first, it survived as a social convention, the

42

same way that shaking hands with the right (that is, the lucky) hand has endured because there was a need for a gesture to represent friendly feelings to a stranger. The week was a short unit of time around which common people could organize their lives, their work, and their leisure. At the same time, the week provided a simple and memorable device for relating everyday activities to supernatural concerns, whether these involved observing a direct commandment from Jehovah, or commemorating Christ's resurrection, or recognizing the influence of a planetary deity, or, just to be safe, all three.

The fact that the week was so adaptable undoubtedly facilitated its worldwide spread. For Constantine, who decreed its use throughout the Roman Empire, the week was a Christian (and some say a Mithraist) institution; for the Hindus, it was a planetary concept that they grafted onto their accommodating, heterogeneous calendar. Early in the seventh century, the week received another religious endorsement, from the prophet Muhammad, who established a lunar calendar that was very different from both the Christian and the traditional Arab calendars. Nevertheless, he kept the seven-day week, although he shifted the holy day from Sunday to Friday.

The last major civilization to jump on the bandwagon was China, where the week arrived as a result of the 1911 Revolution. To the Chinese, the Western calendar was one of many "modernizing" reforms, and the week was adopted pragmatically, and in a curious fashion. Weekdays were numbered, not named; the seventh day was a civic holiday, and was called, in Cantonese, Sun Day. This was probably a matter of convention, not religious conviction, although some political leaders had been educated in mission schools and were, like Sun Yat-sen, the first (provisional) president of the new republic, baptized Christians.

Things went less smoothly for the week during an earlier revolution. The French Revolution produced an entirely revised calendar, whose object was to divorce the months, days, and weeks from their traditional Christian associations and, at the same time, to rationalize (that is, decimalize) timekeeping. To begin with, the republican calendar did away with Anno Domini; henceforth dates were to be reckoned from the proclamation of the republic—1792, or Year I. The solar year was maintained, and the extra day of the leap year was consecrated to a festival of the Revolution, the four-year period being called a *Franciade*. The months, too, were renamed. This task was entrusted to Philippe-François-Nazaire Fabre d'Églantine, a poet, who concocted a sort of twelve seasons—the winter months, for example, were called *nivôse* (snowy), *pluviôse* (rainy), and *ventôse* (windy).*

---

* Typically, for France, this represented Parisian weather.

There were still twelve months, but, as in the civil Egyptian calendar, they were all of equal thirty-day length. The five days left over were devoted to an end-of-the-year public festival.

Under this system the week fared badly—it was done away with altogether. Instead, each month was now divided into three ten-day periods. The days of the revolutionary week, or *décade*, were given numerical designations: *primidi, duodi, tridi,* and so on. The tenth day—*décadi*—was a holiday.

Voltaire wrote that "if you wish to destroy the Christian religion you must first destroy the Christian Sunday," and that was precisely what the secular week set out to do. Since the vast majority of peasants remained believers, one must imagine that celebrations of the Lord's Day, and hence the seven-day count, continued, albeit in secret. The same must have been true for the Jewish Sabbath, especially since the "universal" rights of the revolution did not extend to Jews. But even among confirmed *sans-culottes,* the new week cannot have been popular; it deprived them of sixteen public holidays for which the five festival days did not make adequate recompense. In any event, the ten-day week lasted only until Year XIV, when Bonaparte restored the traditional Gregorian calendar in France.

The French revolutionaries underestimated the potency of the week. This was largely because they misjudged the extent of the religious sentiments of most of the population, for whom the seven-day week and Christianity were inseparable. But they also failed to understand that the week was a deeply held social convention. Ordinary people were prepared to put up with ten-hour days, and hundred-minute hours—in any case, few owned timepieces. The ten-day count, however, was lackluster and mechanical, and had none of the mystery and individual richness of the planetary week. Grounded in an intellectual idea, the new week had no cultural roots, and even had the Jacobins survived, it is unlikely that the *décade* would have persisted.

The most recent attempt to undo the seven-day week occurred in the Soviet Union. In the autumn of 1929, the regime of Joseph Stalin completely restructured the Soviet calendar. The new scheme resembled the French republican calendar in many respects; it, too, had twelve months of thirty days each, the extra days being public holidays. Unlike the French, the Bolsheviks retained the traditional names of the months, for the main target of the reform was the week itself. Henceforth, factories would operate continuously, without a break. There would be no more universal rest day—in fact, no more week at all; workers labored four days, on staggered shifts, and had every fifth day off. This increased the annual number of nonworking days from fifty-two to seventy-two.

The four-day shift may have been less onerous than its six-day Tsarist predecessor but it was unpopular. Since everyone worked on a different schedule, families and friends could seldom enjoy the same day off. Supervisors and managers were obliged to work on many of their free days, so that committee and board meetings could take place. Schools, banks, and administrative offices became disorganized—staff members were never present at the same time. Machinery and equipment were neglected, since no one was personally responsible for their operation. Of course, the abolition of the traditional week was also unpopular with the deeply religious peasants, as well as with the large urban Jewish minority.

The stated purpose of the new calendar was to increase industrial and agricultural production. After less than three years, it became clear that the four-day shift was having the opposite effect, and the five-day week was canceled. Now each month was divided into five weeks of six days each, with every sixth day a common holiday. This arrangement lasted for nine years, when it, too, was abandoned. In June 1940, the Soviet Union returned to the Gregorian calendar and the seven-day week. The official reason given was that a longer week would permit an improvement in factory production, and a reduction of staff. Unofficially, the Bolsheviks would have had to admit their defeat; their campaign to undo the traditional week, the mainstay of the Russian Orthodox Church, had failed.

The week has proved remarkably resilient to such official challenges—as well it might, if one believes that it was ordained by God. Or are we still attracted by the magical properties of the number seven, which continues to find resonances in our collective subconscious? There were seven deadly sins, and seven seas; today we have Snow White and the Seven Dwarfs, the Seven Sisters (elite American women's colleges), and the Group of Seven (Canadian painters). We buy 7-Up at the 7-Eleven. There are also an unusual number of movie titles that include the number seven: *Seven Brides for Seven Brothers, The Seven Year Itch, Seven Beauties,* and *The Seven Samurai* along with its American counterpart, *The Magnificent Seven.* The persistence of the number seven in popular culture attests to the durability of the belief in its magical power.*

There may be another explanation. One of the rhythms that modern biology has identified follows a period of about seven days. These so-called circaseptan rhythms have been detected in several functions of the human body: heartbeat, blood pressure, oral temperature, the acid content of blood, the amount of calcium in the urine, and the quantity of

---

* Nowhere has this belief been carried as far as in Isma'īlianism, a breakaway Islamic sect whose members became known as "Seveners." They believe in seven cycles of history, seven major prophets, and in the coming of the unknown seventh Imam.

cortisol in the adrenal glands. The evidence is incomplete, but it is certainly within the realm of possibility that the seven-day week is an instinctive attempt to establish a social calendar that more or less corresponds to an internal biological fluctuation.

The roots of the week lie deep, too deep to fully understand. An air of mystery surrounds the week; perhaps that, too, is part of its appeal. It is an observance that has been distilled over centuries of use, molded and fashioned through common belief and ordinary usage. Above all, it is a *popular* belief that took hold without magisterial sanction. This, more than anything, explains its durability. Less an intruder than an unofficial guest, the week was invited in through the kitchen door, and has become a friend of the family. A useful friend, for whatever else it did, the seven-day cycle provided a convenient structure for the repetitive rhythm of daily activities; not only a day for worship but also a day for baking bread, for washing, for cleaning house, for going to market—and for resting. Surely this over-and-over quality has always been one of the attractions of the week—and of the weekend? "Once a week" is one of the commonest measures of time. The planetary week is not a grand chronometer of celestial movements or a gauge of seasonal changes; it is something both simpler and more profound: a measure of ordinary, everyday life.

three

A Meaningful Day

The roots of the Sabbath go back at least to the time of Moses. According to the Book of Exodus, the Fourth Commandment enjoined the Jews: "Six days you shall labor, and do all your work; but the seventh day is a Sabbath to the Lord your God, in it you shall not do any manner of work." For the last sixteen hundred years, Christians, too, have set aside one day out of seven as a day free from labor. A similar day is present in Muslim societies. Although the origins of the day of rest are clearly religious, the fact that Hindus, Buddhists, Taoists, and Marxists alike have adopted such a schedule suggests that the weekly break has other resonances in the human condition.

The ancient Greeks did not celebrate Sundays, but they did have many regular festivals, which Plato called breathing spells; he suggested that the gods themselves had appointed festival days, out of pity for toiling humans. The Romans had a similar attitude. "Let contentions of every kind cease on the sacred festivals," wrote Cicero, "and let servants enjoy them with a remission of labor; for this purpose they were appointed at certain seasons." Whether they believe that Sundays (or Saturdays, or Fridays) were ordained by divine intervention or not, most people would agree that the distinguishing characteristic of the weekly day off is that, like any holiday, it is a time without work.

This sounds obvious. Work, after all, dominates the world. "Work and its product, the human artifact," wrote Hannah Arendt, "bestow a measure of permanence and durability upon the futility of mortal life and the fleeting character of human time." Work represents the everyday routine; rest is a temporary interruption. Moreover, the workday appears paramount not only because it dominates the calendar numerically but because it is work that makes rest possible—not the other way around. The weekly day of rest is, in a material sense, a kind of surplus, paid for by labor already completed. Its status is underlined by the way in which we consider the weekend a reward for having worked. "I deserve a holiday," we say after a hard week.

There has never been a human society that did not recognize the need for regular days off, although some have tried to reduce them to a minimum. These spoilsports have usually been regimes that glorified

51

labor and begrudged their citizens the "unproductive" time away from work. During the sixteenth century English Protestant society frowned on the excessive number of traditional nonworking days (Sundays and holy days), of which there were more than two hundred; the second Book of Common Prayer, approved by the English Parliament in 1552, reduced them to seventy-nine. The *décade* of the French revolutionary calendar cut the fifty-two weekly Sunday holidays to thirty-six; the ninety annual days off, as well as the thirty-eight saints' days, were also drastically reduced. The Bolsheviks made a dramatic abbreviation in the number of public holidays, and by instituting the staggered holiday effectively relegated the weekly day of rest to a distinctly inferior status. Probably the most extreme example of a leisureless society was Cambodia in the late 1970s, when the Khmer Rouge turned the entire country into a work camp, and reportedly allowed only every tenth day to be a nonworking day—for the long-suffering citizens of Kampuchea, a breathing spell indeed.

Ancient societies were more generous. The Egyptians proscribed work on a total of about seventy days a year, once every six days on the average. The Athenians celebrated fifty or sixty annual festivals, but in some wealthy Greek city-states this figure was more than three times higher. The Romans in the time of Augustus (27 B.C.–A.D. 14) had sixty-six days off each year, but by the fourth century the number of holidays had been expanded to 175. In Tsarist Russia, there were well over a hundred religious holidays every year, and in some parts of Galicia, where religious festivals followed both the Greek and Roman calendars, the number of nonworking days was reported (in 1909) as exceeding two hundred. In so-called primitive societies, the number of rest days varied. In Hawaii, before American colonization, work was forbidden on more than seventy days. The Hopi Indians of the Southwest reserved more than half the year for leisure. A similar statistic was noted in Ethiopia by a visitor in the early nineteenth century. In Ashanti, now Ghana, the number of holidays reached almost two hundred.

Most North Americans enjoy about 130 days off each year—fifty-two weekends, eleven or twelve public holidays, and about two weeks of personal vacation—which happens to be the historic mean. By contrast, in the People's Republic of China, where Saturday is still a workday and there are only seven public holidays, the number of annual days off is much lower—fewer than seventy.

Anyone who believes that the holiday is a reward for successful work might point out that China is much poorer than the United States, and hence can "afford" fewer days off. The gradual increases in the number of annual holidays in ancient Greece and

Rome suggest that increased wealth allows for more free time. But if days off were a result of prosperity, why did the workingman in industrialized Victorian England have many fewer holidays than did his counterpart in the less affluent Middle Ages? And why, at the turn of the century, when the United States was a much richer country than its neighbor Mexico, did Americans enjoy less than half as many days off as Mexicans, who celebrated 131 public holidays each year? If leisure were tied to prosperity, one would expect that Japan, which has achieved global economic preeminence, would have the largest number of holidays. Not so. A recent study found that the average summer vacation taken by Tokyo residents is 5.2 days, compared with twelve days for New Yorkers.

Of course, the reverse could also be argued, that societies that prosper do so precisely because their citizens work longer. This certainly is at the root of the popular belief that the economic success of the Japanese is linked to a propensity for hard work, or that the poverty of most South American societies is largely the result of long siestas, frequent festivals, and a general preference for merrymaking over work. But while it's true that Brazil and Colombia do have many annual public holidays (twenty-one and seventeen days, respectively), so do Japan (nineteen days) and Israel (fifteen days). No one would seriously suggest that the French standard of living is lower than that of the United States because French family vacations are two and three times longer than those of Americans. Long summer vacations—a tradition in France and West Germany since the 1950s—do not seem to have had any ill effect on the economic growth and prosperity of these two countries. The relationship between the duration of time off and the wealth of a society is not straightforward. The quantity of days off work is neither a simple product of affluence nor a mark of cultural indolence. Its significance lies elsewhere.

In 1914, as part of the war effort, British industry introduced Sunday work, as well as longer hours and overtime. The result was not, as had been hoped, greater production but the opposite: reduced efficiency on the part of the workers, disciplinary difficulties, labor disturbances, and, most surprisingly, an actual drop in overall output. A short time later, when the Sunday holiday was reluctantly reinstated and the twelve-hour day was reduced to ten hours, not only did hourly output increase, to everyone's surprise, but so did gross weekly production.

The implication was obvious—the amount of production was not only a function of how long people worked but also of how long they did not work. Greater attention began to be paid to the effects of the duration of work on productivity, and on the importance of external factors such as fatigue. The chief result of this research was a call for short, intermittent, daily rest periods—which produced, among other things, the coffee break, a sort of Protestant siesta. Since the Sunday holiday was an established tradition that, under normal circumstances, was unlikely to change, little research was done to shed light on the weekly break itself.

The fact that periodic days of rest have existed throughout history suggests that they might be the result of a physiological imperative—that intermittent days off represent a weekly maintenance break, analogous to the body's requirement for a certain number of regenerative hours of sleep or for a given amount of food and water. Such, at least, was the assumption in the nineteenth century, when scientists began to study human fatigue.

Angelo Mosso, an Italian physiologist, published a popular book on fatigue that appeared in English in 1903, in which he described various kinds of fatigue brought on by both physical exertion and by intellectual work, including stressful activities such as writing examinations and lecturing. Mosso drew his evidence from both anecdotal material and his own experiments. He constructed an apparatus that measured the effect of fatigue on muscle strength, which showed that intellectual work also produced a consistent corresponding reduction in physical strength. In the case of one Dr. Maggiora, a professor of medicine who had to administer an arduous series of oral examinations, muscle strength flagged after an afternoon of examining but revived partially after dinner. A night's sleep restored the professor, but another afternoon of examining students brought the same results. After several days, however, the night's rest was no longer enough to return his strength to normal. Following the fifth and final day his forces were, in Mosso's word, "exhausted." As part of the experiment, Dr. Maggiora was then asked to spend two days in the country in "complete idleness." On his return, he demonstrated, as one might expect, a full revival of muscular force. The case of the tired professor showed the recuperative powers of the five-and-two schedule, although two-day weekends were unusual at this time.

We now know that Mosso's thesis—that physical and cerebral fatigue produces a chemical imbalance in the brain—was mistaken, but no simple alternative explanation has presented itself. Medical researchers agree that fatigue has to do with a person's physical and mental state; where the difficulty lies is that the latter "is little reflective and very elemental, almost subconscious by definition, and largely inaccessible to rational analysis," according to one textbook on the subject. Moreover, fatigue at work appears to be the function of a great many associated factors such as working conditions (lighting, ventilation, noise), the degree of worker involvement, and the nature of the work, particularly if it is monotonous. Fatigue remains, in the words of one researcher, "a most mysterious phenomenon." We have not advanced far beyond Mosso's observation that after three or four uninterrupted days at his writing desk, he often had headaches, slept badly, and generally felt tired. At that point, he said, "I shut my books, set aside my papers, and after twenty-four hours' rest I find that I am cured."

Common sense suggests that a periodic day off from our regular occupations is required to combat mental and physical fatigue, stress, and boredom. Although there is no scientific evidence regarding the exact frequency necessary, on the strength of the historical record it would appear that such a break is needed roughly every five to ten days. But we should be careful of jumping to conclusions. A British author, Donald Scott, points out that studies of different industries have shown that output drops to its lowest level at the end of the week, just before the holiday. On the other hand, output is also low at the beginning of the week, when everyone is supposedly rested. He speculates that factors other than fatigue—for example, an improvement in the worker's skill as the week progresses—are at play. But this period of adjustment, for that is what it is, also underlines the essential discontinuity that exists between work and leisure. Jeremy Campbell suggests that the "Monday-morning blahs" are the result of sleeping in on the weekend, which is a way of readjusting the body's twenty-five-hour circadian rhythm to the twenty-four-hour cosmic schedule. On Monday the inner biological clock, which has been allowed to run free, is abruptly brought back into line.

We may require a day off from work to alleviate our fatigue, but to describe holidays only as the antithesis—or consequence—of workdays misses the mark. To call the holiday either an interruption or a reward ignores the wealth of words that have traditionally described the period devoted to leisure—holy day, festival, feast, carnival, celebration—and reduces them to merely two: work stoppage. This is like defining comfort as merely the absence of discomfort; it fails to convey the essential positive quality of the elusive experience. In his book on festivity, Josef Pieper pointed out that the key to grasping the nature of the holiday lay precisely in divorcing it from work and other external influences and goals, and understanding that the holiday is meaningful in itself.

Over time, the meaning of the weekly break has

varied. The carefree modern weekender takes the days of rest as a pleasurable interlude from a hectic work schedule, and also as an opportunity to engage in personal hobbies. He considers the day off as a day when he is not *required* to work (at least, not for others, for the weekend is also a time for household chores); this is different from describing the day off as a day on which one is required *not* to work.

It was the prohibition of work that characterized the earliest regular holidays. An Egyptian calendar that has survived from about 1200 B.C.—the Papyrus Sallier IV—lists a series of forbidden activities for each day or part of a day for the entire year. These include injunctions against travel, sexual intercourse, washing, and eating certain kinds of food. Among the most frequent injunctions is "do no work." A Babylonian calendar, possibly belonging to the age of Hammurabi, describes the seventh, fourteenth, nineteenth, twenty-first, and twenty-eighth days as "evil days," on which various activities were proscribed, including, according to some scholars, business transactions. Unlucky days, on which all important work stopped, were also identified in the Greek and Roman calendars. "Egyptian days," which were considered ill-favored for various activities, were observed in Europe throughout the Middle Ages and until the Reformation. The current prejudice against Friday the thirteenth is a survivor of such superstitions.*

It is often hard to decipher the exact meaning of these ancient customs, but it helps to look at analogous beliefs in "primitive" societies. During the nineteenth century, European travelers made contact with many indigenous cultures in Asia and Africa, where the observance of lucky and unlucky days was actively practiced. The most extreme example was in Polynesia, where everyday life was governed by a vast and complex system of prohibitions, known as *tapus* or *tabus*. These taboos governed people, places, objects, activities, dress, and food, and were supported by supernatural authority. Their violation supposedly resulted in supernatural punishment.

Propitiatory tabooed days could arise as the result of particular events—the outbreak of an epidemic, a natural calamity, or any unusual occurrence. A taboo could occur automatically as the result of a birth, a death, the construction of a house, or before an important hunt. It could also be invoked (by the priest)

---

* Friday has been considered an unlucky day since the Middle Ages, and it remains so in many cultures. Macedonian folk lore proscribes cutting hair and nails on Fridays; Slavic peasants believe that any work begun on the day of "Mother Friday" is bound to finish badly; Indian Brahmins and Parsis consider Friday to be inauspicious, as do the Burmans. Some Islamic societies, which celebrate the Sabbath on Friday, also consider it an unlucky day for certain activities.

as a punishment for a religious or civil transgression, and it could affect an individual, a household, or the entire community. Taboos could last a few days, a few months, or, rarely, several years.

They were also part of everyday life. Traditional Hawaiian religion observed four regular tabooed periods a month: the third through sixth nights, the time of the full moon, the twenty-fourth and twenty-fifth nights, and the twenty-seventh and twenty-eighth nights. During these periods, sexual intercourse was prohibited and various activities—cooking, rowing a canoe, going outside the house—were proscribed.

There were also regularly scheduled seasonal taboos against fishing and hunting, for example, which had a beneficial effect on maintaining food stocks, and on nonagricultural work during the planting and harvesting periods, which ensured that the entire community pitched in for these crucial times. This has led some observers to wonder if taboos had a utilitarian origin, but since identical taboos were imposed on many different occasions, with no apparent practical end in mind, this explanation is unconvincing. If the taboo did serve a practical purpose, it was of a more general kind. Like any belief system, it provided the satisfaction of knowing that one had observed the correct forms. Communal taboos also contributed to a sense of social cohesion and self-discipline, which bound the members of the community together.

The core of the tabooed day was that everyday activities stopped, especially those that involved labor.* Because of this, tabooed days are sometimes called holidays or festivals; as contemporary descriptions make clear, there was nothing festive about them. Work, like certain prized foods, singing, dancing, or sexual intercourse, was forbidden because it could not be safely or beneficially undertaken on these unlucky days. The regularly scheduled tabooed days, which occurred four times a month, resembled the weekend, but the atmosphere of these work breaks was not one of rest and recreation. Fear, not celebration, was their hallmark. These were gloomy days, during which all activities stopped and people stayed at home in an anxious mood of apprehension.

Once the taboo tradition was identified in the South Seas, anthropologists and sociologists found examples of it among indigenous peoples throughout Asia and Africa, and historians identified taboo traditions in the ancient world.† Their recurring features, especially

---

* The Polynesian word *tapu* signifies "specially marked," but *tapua'i* is more explicit and means "to abstain from all work, games, and so on."

† For example, the Romans had special holidays following earthquake tremors, when propitiatory rites were carried out and all public business ceased.

the ban on work, prompted some to point to evidence of taboos in contemporary industrialized societies such as our own. "In economic theory," wrote Thorstein Veblen in his famous book on the leisure class, "sacred holidays are obviously to be construed as a season of vicarious leisure performed for the divinity or saint in whose name the tabu is imposed and to whose good repute the abstention from useful effort on these days is conceived to inure. The characteristic feature of all such seasons of devout vicarious leisure is a more or less rigid tabu on all activity that is of human use."

Discounting Veblen's sly use of "obviously" and "vicarious," his characterization of the prohibition of work on religious holidays as a taboo, and hence as something fundamentally archaic (although probably intended mockingly), was not inaccurate. The Pentateuchal code of the Jews contained many Sabbatarian provisions—not lighting fires or cooking—which most historians agree derived from the taboo beliefs of the Babylonians and Egyptians. The link between the sacred day and the tabooed day was also evident in Polynesia, where New England missionaries tried to introduce a strict observance of Sunday. They were surprised at how easily the natives accepted this foreign practice, not realizing that among their new converts, Sunday was popularly known as *la tabu*.

Veblen's characterization of religious holidays as

tabooed days is misleading, however, for although the holy day undoubtedly borrowed from the earlier taboo tradition, the two were not identical. The holy day emerged as part of the evolution from animism to polytheism, and involved, as the anthropologist Hutton Webster pointed out, a distinction between two contradictory beliefs, that of the "unclean thing" and that of the "holy thing." The former held that work and other secular activities could contaminate the sanctity of the holy day and should be avoided. But at the same time, the day that was consecrated to a divinity was not unlucky—on the contrary, it was considered holy. The observance of its sanctity took the form of various religious rites and rituals, including an abstention from work—not in a spirit of apprehension or atonement but as a form of worship.

Among the Romans, there were two types of holidays, or *feriae:* private family celebrations following a birth, marriage, or death, on which work was proscribed for all (including servants, as Cicero observed); and annual, public *feriae* (of which there were sixty-one in republican times), which were chiefly religious, although some, which fell on *dies religiosi,* were considered merely unlucky (in both cases, work was prohibited). The *feriae* combined elements of both the tabooed and the holy day. With time, the former gave way to the latter. This blending of traditions was not unusual; as Webster observed, it is "a universal tendency of the human mind to dwell with special emphasis on the festive aspects of a holy season, and by some subtle alchemy of the spirit to convert what was once a day of gloom and anxiety into a day of gladness and good cheer."

This conversion of a tabooed day into a holy day is evident in the evolution of the Jewish Sabbath, in which the early, taboo-like proscriptions were replaced (in post-exile times) by a more tolerant attitude that forbade fasting and promoted a more joyous festivity. It became a moral obligation to enjoy oneself on the Sabbath, and the Sabbath meals were occasions for delicacies and special treats. Hymns acclaimed the Sabbath as "a day of rest and joy, of pleasure and delight." This interpretation was in turn replaced by Pharisaic legalism, which tried to reinstate a complex of Sabbatical regulations. It was in opposition to this view that Jesus Christ taught that "the Sabbath was made for man, and not man for the Sabbath." In other words, that it was a rest day for the benefit of mankind, not a tabooed day to be feared.

The early Christians, especially those who were Jews, observed both the Sabbath and the succeeding Lord's Day, when they assembled to break bread. By the time of St. Paul, Sabbath observance was greatly diminished. This did not mean that one replaced the other, though; initially the Lord's Day had few Sabbatarian characteristics. The faithful gathered for the

Eucharist, in commemoration of the Resurrection, but otherwise it was an ordinary working day.

There was another weekly holiday that was different from either the tabooed day, or the holy day—the market day. There was an old tradition among the Romans, perhaps dating back to the Etruscans, that every eighth day was set aside for holding town meetings, conducting public business, and bringing goods to market. The legal character of this day—the nundine (that is, the "ninth day," counting inclusively as the Romans did)—was eventually lost, but the market and leisure function survived. The nundine was a useful device, since ordinary farmers and townspeople, who did not have access to astronomical time-reckoning devices, needed a simple way to schedule public markets. Any interval would have done, as long as it was reasonably short, since food without refrigeration spoiled rapidly in hot climates.

There are two differences between the Roman nundine and our seven-day week. For one thing, the Romans didn't give names to individual days. For another, there was a casualness about the exact length of the period between markets; the nundine was held in different parts of the empire at different intervals, although eight days was the most common.

The eight-day Roman nundine is the oldest known

example of a market week, but it was not unique; analogous periods have been observed in agricultural societies around the world. In West Africa, for example, four-day market weeks were common, and, unlike the nundine, the individual days were usually named; the fifth day was market day, and one more day was set aside as a day of rest. The Akikuyu of East Africa held a market every four days, and in a predetermined rotation in different locations. There were five-day market weeks in Java, Bali, and Sumatra, as well as in ancient Mexico and parts of Central America. In Assam, the market week was eight days long. In pre-Hispanic Colombia, the market week lasted only three days; in Peru, it lasted ten. In old Mexico, markets were held in different villages every four days; sometimes a greater fair was held on every fifth interval, that is, every twenty days, which produced a year of eighteen "market months."

The lengths of the intervals between markets were remarkably consistent—usually between four and eight days, never less than three or more than ten. The main purpose of the market week was to provide a timekeeping device for a regular succession of market days when farmers could gather to exchange goods. But it was more than that. Lacking regular holidays, farmers needed a day of rest. The lives of fishermen and hunters were—and still are—alternations of intensive labor and enforced idleness. The responsibilities of the shepherd or cowherd precluded a day off, but his toil was slight when compared with the exertions of the farmer. Heavy and continuous physical labor—plowing, digging, cultivating, and harvesting—required a regular intermission, and market day provided precisely such a break.

There is explicit evidence for this theory. In Dahomey, in the mid-nineteenth century, every fourth day was a market day and a holiday, "not kept holy, but devoted to the will of the working class; in short, a sort of remuneration to the slave for the three days' labor," observed one British visitor. The tenth day of the Incan week was also a holiday and a market day, which was said (by an old chronicler, himself of Incan descent) to have been conceived "in order that labor might not be so continuous as to become oppressive." Peruvian peasants were required to come to the market to "hear anything that the Inca or his council might have ordained." As in ancient Rome, market day was not only an opportunity for trading and a break from work, it was also a public, social occasion. Goods were exchanged, but so was news, information, and knowledge, for the market gave farmers a chance to break their rural isolation and come into contact with itinerant merchants, tinkers, and entertainers.

The seven-day week has replaced the market week in most of these societies, but the market day persists.

I have attended markets in the town of Benue, in central Nigeria, where despite the presence of video-cassettes and plastic buckets, the atmosphere was much as it must have been in the past: a holiday, characterized by loud trading, gossip, music, and playfulness. The open-air bazaar had not the least resemblance to the scrubbed solemnity of the modern supermarket but reminded me instead of a garage sale or a church rummage sale—or, for that matter, of a seasonal country fair of the type that is still held in American and Canadian rural towns and villages.

The first Sunday law can be dated with certainty. In A.D. 321, the Emperor Constantine decreed that, throughout the Roman Empire, magistrates, city people, and artisans were to abstain from work "on the venerable day of the Sun." He pointedly exempted farmers from this obligation, since there was a Roman tradition that even on *feriae* necessary agricultural work was permitted. Historians disagree on whether this legislation was the result of Constantine's Christianity, his acknowledgment of the growing acceptance of the planetary week, or his recognition of the popularity of Mithraism. In any case, there was no mention of the Lord's Day, neither then nor four months later, when the strict law was amended to permit various public acts, since "it seemed unworthy of the day of the sun, honored for its own sacredness, to be used in litigations and baneful disputes."

The first imperial edict to specifically mention the

Lord's Day was issued sixty years after Constantine's decree. As Christianity spread, the Christian Sunday assimilated the day of the sun and became a civic holiday, free from work. At the same time, the ecclesiastical authorities began to proscribe various Sunday activities. In 436, the Fourth Council of Carthage, for instance, discouraged Sunday attendance at games and circuses, although it did not ban them outright; the Third Council of Orléans judged it "better to abstain" from all rural work, "so that people may the more readily come to the churches and have leisure for prayers."

The term "Christian Sabbath" was first used in the twelfth century, and it marks the beginning of the church's grafting of the Sabbatarian tradition onto the Lord's Day. It became a mortal sin to do any unnecessary work on Sunday, as the clergy, with the help of civil laws, attempted to drape a pall of Pharisaic gloom over the day. In practice, though, Sunday was still a festive day. Part of Constantine's edict had involved shifting the nundine from the eighth day to the day of the sun, and this tradition continued strongly in many parts of medieval Europe, in spite of clerical attempts to forbid it.* The reemergence of Sunday shopping (mainly in the United States, and more gradually in Canada) is a return to this market tradition.

---

* This tradition is recalled by the Hungarian word for Sunday, which means "market day."

Medieval Sundays were both holy days and civic holidays; work was generally forbidden, but other activities took place, including sporting events, tourneys, plays, pageants, festivals, feasts, parish ales (where much of the substance was consumed), and various other public amusements. The day happily combined the social recreations of the market day and the celebratory, religious festivity of the Sabbath—as so often happened in the Middle Ages, the secular and the profane merged one into the other. In any event, Sunday was only one holy day among a multitude of festivals and saints' days, and did not carry the full weight of religious observance.

The character of Sunday was greatly altered by the Reformation. Some, like Calvin, considered that religious services could be held on any day of the week; although he did preserve holy Sunday as a practical measure, Calvin himself bowled after services. Others placed the Sunday service—and so the entire day—at the center of religious life. "Everything is governed and ordained by the Gospel, baptism, and Sunday prayer," preached Martin Luther. Sunday was the occasion not only for devotions but for instruction; most Lutheran adults attended catechism classes after church.* The day acquired a wholly religious

---

* The Counter-Reformation, too, stressed attendance at Sunday Mass and, by the eighteenth century, Sunday vespers as well.

character, and, given the inclination of the Protestant faiths for seriousness and simplicity, it also lost its medieval gaiety. This character found its ultimate expression not on the Continent but in England, where Puritans (and, to a lesser extent, the Church of England) eventually made Sunday into a gloomy festival, a veritable tabooed day.

Before the Reformation, Sunday churchgoing had been a religious, not a civic obligation. In 1551, the British Act of Uniformity made absence from Sunday services punishable by a fine. The Sunday Observance Act of 1677 went further and forbade "tradesmen, artificers, and laborers" from carrying out any business. This law was applied in the widest possible way and prohibited even boatmen from plying their trade. In 1781, a law was passed that made it a serious offense to hold any form of public entertainments on Sundays for which people were charged an entrance fee. This ban stayed in force for 150 years. As late as 1856, when free Sunday band concerts began to take place in London parks, the Archbishop of Canterbury objected, and they were stopped. That same year, the House of Commons refused to consider a suggestion that the National Gallery and the British Museum stay open on Sunday afternoons.

It was not surprising that English settlers, many of whom were Puritans, brought their strict Sunday customs to the colonies. The first Sunday law enacted by the Colony of Virginia, in 1610, enjoined all men and women to attend divine services in the morning and catechism in the afternoon. The penalty for a first offense was losing a week's provisions; for the second offense, whipping; and, for the third, death. The latter punishment was unusual, but laws requiring attendance at Sunday services and prohibiting work, travel, sports, and other frivolous pastimes also existed in Maryland, Massachusetts, and Connecticut. They became a distinguishing feature of all the new American colonies—the Carolinas as well as New York, Pennsylvania, New Hampshire, Maine, and New Jersey.

"Blue laws"—named after the blue paper on which a Sunday edict had been written in New Haven in 1781—were widespread. Although a strict Puritan interpretation of blue laws lapsed after the War of Independence, the Sabbatarian tradition has continued to the present day. It remains strongest in states such as Massachusetts and Maryland, but, as late as 1985, thirty-nine states continued to restrict Sunday activities, either by a general ban on all commerce and labor (twenty-two states) or by restrictions on specific activities. The latter make a curious list. Every Sunday, somewhere in the United States, it is illegal to barber; bowl; play billiards, bingo, polo, or cards; gamble; race horses; hunt; go to the movies; sell cars, fresh meat or alcohol; organize boxing or wrestling matches; hold public dances or sporting events; or dig oysters.

"The festive quality of a holiday depends on its being exceptional," wrote Josef Pieper. I can recall my own childhood Sundays as days apart from the rest of the week. To begin with, we slept in, and breakfast was later than usual. Like my parents, my brother and I put on special clothes—our Sunday best. We went to church, which took most of the morning and established the mood for the rest of the day—not necessarily one of sanctity but of singularity. What I remember more clearly than Sunday Mass is the ride home after church, the pleasurable feelings of satisfaction that a serious obligation had been fulfilled (and sin averted) and the relief that this serious part of the day was over.

Sunday lunch was also special; at least, it was an occasion for special food. Not roast beef and Yorkshire pudding—my parents' Anglophilia did not extend that far—but more elaborate dishes than on a weekday. Sunday lunches were also the occasion for guests, when my father, with some ceremony, placed wine on the table. I realize now that this "Sabbath meal" was really a celebration, and hence an implicit part of the holiness of the day.

Sunday the family stayed at home. I don't recall

Sunday afternoon drives, although there must have been some, at least when I was a youngster and automobile ownership was still a novelty. Sometimes we children bicycled to the Yacht Club (despite the grand name, there were no boats—the river pier was used only for swimming), where there were tennis courts.

There was a final punctuation before Sunday was over—*The Ed Sullivan Show*. We watched it religiously. The word is not altogether inappropriate, for in addition to acrobats, jugglers, and comics, there was usually a "serious" act, a choir or a dramatic reading, which tempered the burlesque atmosphere and was, I think, an implicit recognition of the special day. This was family entertainment, but it was also Sunday entertainment, and the host's notoriously delicate sense of decorum was influenced by the latter as much as it was by the former.

Ed Sullivan—like most of what we saw on television—had the added exoticism of being foreign, for we lived in Canada. Or more precisely, in Quebec, French Canada, which was predominantly Roman Catholic. Catholicism traditionally imposed few of the Sunday inhibitions of Protestantism—most European Catholic countries, for example, never instituted Sunday laws.* This was not the case in Quebec,

---

* In Spain, for instance, bullfights are traditionally held on Sunday afternoons.

however, which came under English Sunday legislation in 1774 during the reign of George III, but since the ordinances were never strictly enforced, Sunday traditions were more relaxed there than in the rest of Canada.

The difference in Sunday observance between French and English Canada went unnoticed until it was dramatically underlined during the vociferous 1906 countrywide debate on national Sunday legislation. The conflict between Catholic Quebec and Protestant Ontario—the chief protagonists—recalled the arguments that had divided papists and Puritans in seventeenth-century England. The Protestant Lord's Day Alliance wanted to put an end not only to all Sunday commerce but to Sunday streetcars, rail travel, and "public spectacles." But the prime minister, Sir Wilfred Laurier, the first French Canadian to hold that office, told a Protestant Member of Parliament, "In the province of Quebec we have a different way of observing the Sabbath, and I am not pretending that we observe it in a better fashion than other people. Everybody in our province goes to church in the morning, and in the afternoon he is at liberty to engage in those contests. The young people play baseball, which I know is objectionable to some Christian communities. For instance, in the constituency of my honorable friend it would be a high moral offense for a young man to play ball on a Sunday."

As has happened so often in Canadian history, the resolution of this cultural conflict was a compromise. The Dominion Lord's Day Act was passed in full, but an amendment was added that left enforcement to the discretion of the provincial attorneys general and that furthermore allowed the provinces to pass modifying legislation. In Quebec, this made the federal Sunday law a dead letter.

As in the past, neither sports nor public entertainments were banned in Quebec, and although large businesses like offices and factories were closed, small shops could stay open. The day had some of the features of the festive medieval Sunday, and, as in the Middle Ages, the church frowned on this levity. In 1922, inspired by a pastoral letter decrying the lax observance of Sunday as a day of rest, the Ligue du Dimanche (Sunday League) was formed. For fourteen years the League agitated for Sabbatarian legislation, particularly against cinemas, but politicians, sensing the public mood, resisted efforts to impose stricter rules, and the province remained the only place in Canada where movie theaters stayed open on Sunday.*

---

* The Sunday League's chief success—and it was a shameful one—was to force the abrogation of that part of the law that had permitted Jews to carry on their business on Sunday. This was the result of a general anti-Semitic climate that existed in Quebec during the 1920s and 1930s.

The contradictions between Sunday legislation, the lenient application of laws, and the strict teaching of the clergy continued in Quebec for several decades. When I was a boy growing up there in the 1950s, I could go to movies and sporting events on Sunday; had I been older, I could have bought a drink in a restaurant, or (illegally) a bottle of beer at the accommodating corner store. At the same time, the atmosphere was not one of unbridled gaiety—the parish priest saw to that. Except for morning churchgoers, the streets were empty, as empty as the clotheslines awaiting the Monday wash. People avoided being seen doing yardwork or household chores; there were no Sunday papers.

I remember Sunday as an idle day—no housework was done, no vacuuming or clothes washing, no digging in the garden. This custom was not followed strictly, for I was asked, one Sunday, to mow the front lawn. An earnest catechism student, I knew this sort of work was forbidden, and as a prim adolescent I was scandalized by what the neighbors would think of this flagrant, public flaunting of the day of rest. As I pushed the mower over the small patch of grass I imagined secret eyes behind drawn curtains—I might as well have been made to wear a scarlet letter.

My childhood Sunday was not the festive celebration of the Middle Ages, the somber holiday of the Puritans, or the unlucky day of the Polynesians.

Or, rather, it was all three: a curious combination of day of rest, holy day, and tabooed day. This amalgam of traditions suggests that in one form or another, Sunday—or whatever name we choose to give this meaningful day—will continue to punctuate the course of time. It may evolve into more of a rest day, an introspective retreat from the busy workweek, not because of physical exhaustion but out of mental fatigue or boredom. If material pleasures wane, it could reaffirm its religious, celebratory function. Or it could become more secular—Sunday at the mall, not Sunday with the catechism, a market day instead of a tabooed day.

four

Sunday in the Park

There have been scores of Sunday painters, but there is one great Sunday painting: Georges Seurat's *A Sunday on the Grande Jatte.* For six months, beginning in the late spring of 1884, the young artist went daily to the Île de la Grande Jatte to work on studies and sketches for the final painting. During the week he concentrated on the landscape elements that formed the background to his subject. One can imagine him shifting his attention on Sunday, when the previously empty park filled up with crowds of holidaying Parisians.

The island of Grande Jatte lies in the middle of the Seine, upstream from Asnières and Clichy, where the river loops around to encircle the northwest edge of Paris. Today this area is completely citified, the skyline dominated by the futuristic architecture of the nearby La Défense, but in the nineteenth century it was the site of a different type of modern novelty— the suburb. The Parisian suburbs, or *banlieues,* were a result of the rebuilding of the city that had been undertaken in the 1850s, during the Second Empire. The boulevards and avenues that were cut through working-class neighborhoods in the center of Paris displaced many people. When the new railways made it possible to live outside the encircling fortifications that had traditionally defined the city, many—including the working poor—moved there. At the same time, industrialization was attracting people to the city from the countryside; by 1900 Paris would have 2.5 million inhabitants. The physical expansion occurred in concentric rings: first, closest to the city, were the industrial slums of the workers; next, slightly farther out, the tidy houses of the middle class; lastly, at the perimeter, beyond the reach of the railway (and hence of the masses), one found the fashionable homes of the *haute bourgeoisie*.

The better residential suburbs of Paris were in the south; to the north of the city, the suburbs were mainly industrial. Such was Clichy, on the main railway line to the Channel ports and served by the barges that plied the Seine. The town contained workshops and factories, a smoke-belching gasworks, as well as rows of squalid tenements. Asnières, across the river, was a *petit-bourgeois* residential area, half-country, half-town. The narrow island of Grande Jatte lay between the two. Too small to be of practical use, it had been left in its natural wooded state, and had become, as Richard Thomson described it, a "no-man's land, between bourgeois propriety and proletarian dereliction."

Throughout the second half of the nineteenth century, Grande Jatte was a favorite destination for Parisians who wanted to spend a day in the country, or at least in a countrylike setting. It had been first a boating center, later a place for strolling and picnics. The location was convenient for short excursions, only two and a half miles by train from the Gare Saint-Lazare; those who lived near the Place de l'Étoile could take a horse-drawn omnibus straight down the Avenue de Neuilly. For the adventurous, the velocipede was an alternative, and if they could afford a new bicycle, with the pneumatic tires made by the Michelin brothers, it was a comfortable ride.

Like many Parisian painters, Georges Seurat was attracted to the outer suburbs and their peculiarly odd mixture of images—pastoral and industrial, field and factory. This interest started early; his father owned property in the northeast suburbs, and some of Seurat's earlier drawings were made there. In 1881, when he was twenty-two, suburban subjects began to appear in his work, and two years later he started to make regular painting excursions to Asnières. Seurat probably took the train, since he lived in Montmartre, not far from the Gare Saint-Lazare.

Seurat's first major painting was the masterful

Bathing, Asnières, which shows a group of young men swimming in the Seine. Some are in the water; others sit or recline on the grassy bank. The mood is summery. The island of Grande Jatte can be seen in the background, its verdure contrasting with the bridge and the smoking factory chimneys of Clichy on the far shore. Despite the clash of images, however, there is no social comment. Without irony, Seurat, a bourgeois, represented a *petit-bourgeois* scene. The swimmers in the scene, judging from their clothes—bowler hats, a straw boater, white shirts, elastic-sided boots—and their decorous postures, are not factory hands. They are store clerks or office workers, inhabitants of Asnières who have come to the grassy riverbank after work for the fresh air and relaxation, for a swim, to enjoy the view of the pleasure boats on the water. This is a portrayal of the suburb as a setting for leisure.

Seurat began work on his next painting immediately. This time he chose a location directly across the river, on the island itself. *Sunday on the Grande Jatte,* completed in 1886, was more ambitious both in the choice of theme and in its composition. On the riverbank, among young trees, whose long afternoon shadows dapple the ground, Seurat disposed many human figures—men, women, and children. Some were walking, some standing, some sitting on the grass. Most were facing the water, gazing across at Asnières on the far shore. The small stretch of river glimpsed through the trees was no less crowded and included several sailboats, a rowboat, a four-man scull, a steam launch, a tug, and the Asnières ferry, with a tricolor at its stern.

Seurat crammed his large (six and a half by ten feet) canvas with more than forty figures. One woman stands beside the water, hand on hip, holding a fishing pole; nearby, a girl and a man are posed motionless, like statues, at the water's edge. A couple holds an infant in swaddling clothes. Two soldiers stroll side by side; a little girl in a white dress primly accompanies her nanny; a dumpy figure in a wet nurse's bonnet sits mutely with a companion, paying no notice to the nearby solitary man playing a trumpet. The atmosphere is sunny but lethargic—a dog-day afternoon. The sense of movement is arrested, and yet so strongly implied that for the modern viewer it is like watching a movie in which the film speed has been turned down almost to zero and the action unfolds imperceptibly, frame by frame.

Seurat's methodical technique and careful composition—he made three preparatory canvases, thirty painted studies, and about twenty-six drawings—went well with his choice of subject: a Sunday scene of bourgeois decorum and propriety. Or is that too simple a reading? "The *Grande Jatte* is one of those great pictures in which every generation finds the meaning best suited to it," wrote John Russell. For many, the painting's significance lies in its delicate rendering of light, its masterful composition of simplified forms, and, of course, its pointillist technique. When the painting was first shown, many critics considered Seurat's style too primitive, verging on caricature. Others felt this was intentional; the painter was satirizing his subject. "The painting has tried to show the toing and froing of the banal promenade that people in their Sunday best take, without any pleasure, in the places where it is accepted that one should stroll on a Sunday," wrote Alfred Paulet in his review of the Eighth Impressionist Exhibition, where *Grande Jatte* was first shown. "The artist has given his figures the automatic gestures of lead soldiers moving about on regimented squares." Since there is no record of any explanation of the painting by its maker, the viewer must decide for himself whether Seurat is mocking these Sunday promenaders or merely observing them. It is revealing that the title he himself gave to his painting was so specific, not only as to the location (which was not unusual) but also as to the day of the week. In *A Sunday on the Grande Jatte,* Seurat dealt deliberately, and in great detail, with a subject that fascinated him, as it did many of his contemporaries: the nature of popular urban leisure in an industrial age.

Seurat portrayed a scene whose ingredients are recognizably modern: escaping the city for an afternoon, walking in the park, sitting on the grass, sailing on the river, fishing by the shore, taking pets for a stroll. The languid Sunday atmosphere, too, is unmistakable. Update the costumes, take away the parasols, add some boys playing with a Frisbee and a teenager lugging a boombox, and this could be Central Park, or Mount Royal in Montreal, on a summer Sunday afternoon.

More than a hundred years have passed since *Grande Jatte* was painted, and, in some ways, not much has changed. This would not be true if we traveled a further hundred years back. Hugh Cunningham, a British historian, wrote, "In 1780 no one could have predicted the shape of leisure a century ahead. In 1880, by contrast, the lines of development are clear . . . There is nothing in the leisure of today which was not visible in 1880."

What happened, according to Cunningham, was the so-called Industrial Revolution. It is common to consider this a cataclysmic occurrence, a watershed, with the modern world on one side and preindustrial society on the other. Such a view can be misleading, however. The term "Industrial Revolution" itself, popularized by Arnold Toynbee, implies sudden and dramatic change, whereas industrialization was a process, one that lasted a hundred years or so. The changes that took place in the period between 1780 and 1880 were the result not only of industrial inventions but also of social and commercial innovations, many of which had occurred earlier.

But Cunningham is right about one thing: by the 1880s, when Seurat was painting his suburban scenes, leisure had assumed a character that could be called modern. A hundred years earlier, it had had a different form. How did this evolution occur? Let's go back to the period immediately before industrialization began, the first half of the eighteenth century, to England, where industrialization first appeared, and take a look at the nature of popular leisure.

This period, roughly 1700 to 1750, was a time of great prosperity for England, which had replaced Spain and Portugal as the world's dominant sea power, hence commercial power. The economy boomed; goods flowed to Britain from India, Asia, the West Indies, and North America, as well as from the Continent, which still accounted for the biggest share of England's trade. Since affluence is a prerequisite for leisure, we would expect this to be a time when the pursuit of pleasure was given importance. Expenditures on the home increased dramatically and produced an extraordinarily refined domestic architecture, pottery and porcelain of unparalleled elegance, a generation of furniture makers whose work continues to be prized, and the eighteenth-century garden.

What was novel about the early eighteenth century was that this prosperity was widespread—or at least more widespread than before. The "leisured classes" included not only the aristocracy and the landed gentry but also the middle class. It was the latter who inhabited the Georgian terrace houses and who were the patrons of Chippendale, Hepplewhite, and Wedgwood.

Nothing characterized this new age better than the growth in popularity of three luxury goods: coffee, tea, and tobacco. Coffee had been introduced to England in the 1650s and had quickly become fashionable—by 1700 there were two thousand coffeehouses in London alone. Tea, which arrived at about the same time, took longer to catch on, as it was expensive; but when trade from the Far East increased, and prices fell, tea consumption increased enormously. Eventually tea became cheaper than coffee, and much cheaper than chocolate, another fashionable drink. Twenty thousand pounds of tea were imported in 1700; sixty years later it was 5 *million* pounds (that was the official figure—probably an equal amount arrived illegally from France). The third popular "poison" of the time—for so it was that many contemporary critics considered these products—was tobacco, which was smoked, chewed, and taken as snuff.

Coffee, tea, and tobacco had all been known before, but during the early eighteenth century, consumption surged on the Continent as in England. Why these three substances should have been received with such enthusiasm at this particular time is hard to explain. The French historian Fernand Braudel has suggested that coffee, tea, and tobacco, which are all stimulants, were meant to compensate for dietary deficiencies. This may have been the case in France and Germany but was hardly true in England, where caloric intake was generally high, and even less so in prosperous Holland, the country that had introduced tea to the English, and a nation then famous for overeating. Another, more likely explanation is that the new popularity of coffee, tea, and tobacco reflected the growing availability of leisure time. They were not, after all, dietary staples: all three were—and are—associated with relaxation and "taking a break" from work.

The increase in consumption of such luxuries was the result of the prosperity of many individuals, encouraged by the increased marketing skills of entrepreneurs. Napoléon later dismissed the British as a nation of shopkeepers; they would have been better described as a nation of customers. That is the most striking thing about early-eighteenth-century leisure, not merely that it was enjoyed by many but that it gave many the opportunity to consume a wide variety of both material goods and culture. "The cultural poverty of late-seventeenth-century England was vast," writes the eminent historian J. H. Plumb. "No newspapers, no public libraries, no theaters outside London, no concerts anywhere, no picture galleries of any kind, no museums, almost no botanical gardens, and no organized sports." During the next hundred years, all this changed.

The number of people who read for pleasure is a good indicator of leisure, since reading requires the availability of not only money but, more important, time. What people read, in addition to newspapers (the first English daily was founded in 1702), were magazines. The magazine was a Georgian invention, and there were dozens of them. Most were of general interest, such as *The Gentleman's Magazine, The Lady's Magazine, The Tatler, The Rambler, The Idler,* and the famous *Spectator* (a daily); in addition, there were magazines that dealt with such specialized subjects as fashion, music, and gardening. The most successful monthlies did not have large circulation by modern standards—only about ten thousand copies—but their readership far exceeded this number, since bound copies were available in coffeehouses and taverns, or for a small fee from so-called newsrooms, as well as from the circulating libraries that were becoming common in the provinces.

The magazine was a product specifically designed for leisure. Like the newspaper, it informed: but it also entertained. It was more opinionated than its modern descendants, and was often written entirely by one person: in the case of *The Rambler* and later *The Idler,* Samuel Johnson; Daniel Defoe produced three issues of *The Review* each week. Magazines contained essays, political views, advice on self-improvement, fashion plates, social satire, gossip, and serialized fiction. It was this last, as published in *The Spectator,* that is generally considered to be the precursor of the eighteenth century's greatest literary innovation—the novel.

The novel derived its form—and its name—from northern Italy, but first achieved prominence in the English language in the 1740s. Samuel Richardson's *Pamela* and *Clarissa,* Tobias Smollett's *Roderick Random,* and Henry Fielding's *Joseph Andrews* and *Tom Jones* all appeared in that decade, and introduced the genre to an immediately enthusiastic reading public. The novel was, from the first, a commercial venture. *Pamela,* arguably the first modern English novel, and its author's first literary effort, was commissioned by two London printers. It was a great success and went through four editions in six months; in true entrepreneurial spirit, Richardson produced a sequel. With an eye to the market, eighteenth-century printers devised the "part-book," which reduced the price of each book for the poorer reader—of whom there were many—and also increased profits, always assuming the public was hooked. This was how the immensely popular *Clarissa* appeared—two volumes the first year, two the next, and the last three just in time for the following Christmas. Another example of part-book publishing was Laurence Sterne's *Tristram Shandy,* which appeared in nine volumes over a period of eight years.

There is no more leisurely occupation than reading a novel. It requires calm surroundings, a comfortable chair, and long periods of uninterrupted time. Magazines and newspapers could be read in noisy coffee-houses, but the novel was a different creature. It signaled the arrival of a new type of leisure activity—introverted, intimate, personal, and private—and undoubtedly accounted for the growth of domesticity during this period.

Widespread private leisure was a thing of the future, however, and most entertainments were still public. The eighteenth century saw an explosive growth in the number of playhouses, both in the large cities and in smaller provincial towns. Between 1700 and 1750 more than a thousand new plays were produced; nor was attendance limited to the rich, as the popularity of cheaper "after-hours" performances shows. The general public was also provided with comic opera, pantomime, and puppet theater. In the second half of the century, the number of theaters continued to increase dramatically, and the quantity of new plays doubled.

New popular entertainments were devised, the most striking of which was the circus. The word circus comes from Charles Hughes's "Royal Circus," an enclosed amphitheater which was built in 1782, but the real inventor of the circus was Philip Astley, who presented the first circus performance in 1768. Astley was an equestrian, but he soon expanded his show to include pantomime, tumbling, acrobats, and clowns. His circus was based in London; the winter was spent performing in Paris, under the patronage of the queen, Marie Antoinette. Soon there were permanent circus buildings in all the large cities and, by 1800, there were dozens of smaller, traveling troupes—usually run by people trained by Astley— that took the spectacle to the provinces.

A parallel popularization occurred in music, with the introduction of musical societies and subscription concerts. The first regular public concerts in London had begun in 1672, organized by John Bannister, a violinist. A few years later, Thomas Britton, a coal merchant, converted a loft in his warehouse into a "concert room" and presented weekly recitals that attracted notable performers (among them Handel) and introduced the London public to the music of such Continental favorites as Vivaldi. Taverns and inns often had small music rooms, and by the middle of the eighteenth century there were many famous locales such as the York Buildings and Hickford's, where the young Mozart played. Eventually larger halls were built that were no longer improvised spaces but designed especially for musical performances.

Concerts and plays were operated as a business, and, like all commercial entertainments, they needed publicity. This the newspapers and the magazines provided, not only in the form of reviews but also through advertising, another Georgian innovation. "Puffery," as it was derisively called by its critics, played a key role in the popularization of public leisure by attracting the public to theater and music—and new books—and by promoting sporting events.

The popularity of horse racing, for example, grew, thanks largely to newspapers, which not only advertised races but carried news of the results. The early 1700s saw a local recreation turn into a national industry: the Jockey Club, established in 1725, enforced standard rules; the Racing Calendar regulated meetings nationwide; the General Stud Book documented pedigrees. Another sport that became popular during this period was cricket. Although a version of the game had been played two hundred years earlier, the first definite match of which there is a record was in 1700. This record, aptly enough, is to be found in *The Post Boy,* the first nonofficial commercial London newspaper. Newspaper advertising played an important role in publicizing cricket matches, which eventually attracted large crowds—not because the game was a rousing spectacle but because it was particularly suited to gambling, both for stake money and for continuous side bets. The game itself was also highly commercialized—many of the players were professionals, paid from subscriptions raised from cricket club members, from prize money, and from gate receipts (unlike horse-racing courses, which had unrestricted access, cricket grounds were usually fenced). The promoters of the sport were entrepreneurs such as Thomas Lord, who established the famous cricket ground that still bears his name, and innkeepers like George Smith, who ran the Artillery Ground where crowds of up to twenty thousand paid tuppence a head to eat, drink, wager, and noisily amuse themselves.

If one had to choose a characteristic Georgian recreation, though, it wouldn't be cricket or novel reading but animal baiting. Blood sports were hardly invented in the eighteenth century; cockfighting had arrived in England a hundred years earlier, and bearbaiting was older than that. But the same commercial forces that impelled the growth of theater, reading, and horse racing also advanced the popularity of the cockpit and the bear garden. Just as innkeepers provided premises for social clubs, musical and theatrical evenings, political societies, even libraries, they also were pleased to maintain locales for prizefights and for a variety of blood sports.

Here was an opportunity for a crowd of men—

public leisure was still mainly a male preserve—to drink, shout, wager, and revel in the sight and smell of blood. Even more than wrestling and prizefighting, which were also popular, contests between animals (cocks and dogs) and between dogs and an unfortunate bear, badger, or bull fascinated the public, rich and poor.

Undoubtedly the chance to wager had a lot to do with it, for, like all prosperous societies, this was a betting society. The excitement of the spectacle was also an attraction; the Georgian public was by all accounts an impassioned one, whether it was rallying behind Richard Nyren, Hambledon's leading cricketer, or cheering a bird in one of the cockpits on London's Birdcage Walk.

What contributed mightily to the excitement was the consumption of alcohol, mainly cheap gin. It has been estimated that between 1700 and 1735 the annual amount of gin legally produced in England grew from four hundred thousand gallons to more than 4 million; to this must be added the considerable output of illicit gin shops, and homemade stills.

The popularization of gin, brandy, rum, and a host of other grain alcohols throughout Europe was the result of eighteenth-century technological developments in distillation, which reduced the cost of production and allowed alcohol to be distilled from a variety of local, inexpensive, fermentable materials:

rye, wheat, corn, barley, sugarcane, potatoes, apples, and many other common fruits. In England, the rapid rise in the consumption of gin—and later rum—was aided by the business acumen of tavernkeepers, who discovered the profitable symbiosis between drinking, betting, and public sports.

The first half of the eighteenth century saw the beginning of what J. H. Plumb has called the "commercialization of leisure," a trend that would continue throughout the Georgian and Victorian epochs. What's striking about this commercialization is it didn't mean, as one might expect, the commercialization of traditional or amateur recreations. It was businessmen who promoted the growth of cricket, music, circuses, theater, magazines, novels, and horse racing. This is worth pointing out, since our conventional view holds that commercial leisure activities—and today almost all leisure has a commercial component—are somehow a crass distortion of "pure" leisure.

Public houses and taverns were important centers of public leisure, whether they were promoting prizefights, cricket matches, or musical concerts. There was one inevitable problem, however, with the otherwise happy combination of commerce and play: excessive drinking. As Fernand Braudel put it, "By the early eighteenth century, the whole of London society, from top to bottom, was determinedly getting drunk on gin." Drunkenness reached unprecedented heights in the eighteenth century and had many adverse effects—not only public disorder and rowdiness, and familial misery, but also a generally poor state of health. The high mortality rates that characterized this period were due in no small part to the immoderate consumption of spirits, especially homemade spirits, which were often poisonous.*

The reason for the popularity of spirits was their extremely low price—unlike beer, they were taxed only lightly. Desultory efforts were made in the 1730s to tax alcohol—desultory because the outcome was widespread rioting. In 1751, the Gin Act raised the tax and imposed controls on retail sales by distillers. This did have a dampening effect on consumption, but it wasn't until a hundred years later, when Gladstone imposed extremely heavy taxes on spirits, that popular consumption of alcohol diminished and beer drinking regained its traditional primacy.

Since drinking was intimately linked to so many recreational activities, the condemnation by social reformers and church groups of the former led to dis-

---

* Drinking on the job was customary, and remained so until the middle of the nineteenth century. Nor was it done secretly—a bottle was generally purchased communally, and different trades had different drinking traditions: printers preferred rum; tailors favored gin.

approval of the latter; before the mid-nineteenth century, sporting events and athletics in general were not considered respectable by the middle class. Blood sports, in particular, became a target of religious and social reformers, although it took many years before laws were passed prohibiting bearbaiting (1835) and cockfighting (1849). Prizefighting, too, was under attack, though it persisted even longer; the Queensberry Rules, forbidding bare-knuckle pugilism, were adopted only in 1866. Of course, this did not mean these activities died out immediately—in fact they continued illicitly—but they did diminish.

Horse racing, which provided many chances for wagers, was appropriated by the upper classes for their own amusement rather than being banned. The improvised country races often staged by tavern-keepers were replaced by large organized events on permanent tracks. A 1740 Act of Parliament restrained the number of small local races and promoted the sport among the aristocrats. They became its chief patrons, breeding the horses, hiring the professional jockeys, and making races such as the St. Léger, the Derby, and the Oaks—which were all founded in the 1770s and would become part of the five "classics"— into important social occasions. At the same time, formal public betting came into existence at several tracks, which further encouraged the involvement of the lower classes, who, if they did not have access to the boxes of the rich, could at least mingle with the toffs and nobs at trackside.

The appropriation of popular sports by the wealthy continued in the nineteenth century. Professional touring cricket teams were replaced by an organization of county teams, which consisted of upper- and middle-class players, all amateurs. The dominance of county cricket, which occurred in the period 1860–80, was literal—the amateurs simply outplayed the professionals. This was a result of the introduction of cricket to the exclusive Victorian public (i.e., private) schools. Amateur cricket turned a raucous and noisy sport into a polite pastime for gentlemen. Beginning in the 1840s, football, previously a workingman's pastime, started to become an upper-class sport. The rules were altered and formally codified and eventually the game (now called rugby) came to be adopted in this form by many of the public schools. The traditional version of the game, in which the ball cannot be picked up, became known as association football, or soccer, and remained the proletarian favorite.

The nineteenth century saw the increasing privatization of leisure by the middle classes, who elevated the status of the home to a previously unimagined level, spent large amounts of money on architecture and decoration, and spent much of their free time in a domestic atmosphere. Around the same time, another leisure institution made its appearance. Belonging to a private club, for men, was also a way of keeping the crowd at bay. The changes in such sports as horse racing, cricket, and football all reflected a general desire on the part of the better-off to distance themselves from the general population.

But leisure was also a way of asserting status in a public way—hence the popularity of such pastimes as fox hunting and shooting, which by law and custom were unavailable to ordinary people. The pastime of yachting, which grew in popularity during the first half of the nineteenth century, was ideally suited to conspicuous consumption. It was expensive, hence exclusive. The yachtsman could distance himself from the crowd simply by sailing out into the middle of a lake—there was no need for fences or enclosures. At the same time, it was—and remains—a gratifying opportunity to be seen, admired, and envied by the plebeians on the shore.

The segregation of leisure according to social class was not wholesale, however, and during the mid-Victorian period there were several opposing influences. One was the rational recreation movement. Initially a middle-class phenomenon that promoted circulating libraries, literary societies, and public lectures, it eventually turned its attention to the public at large. The general idea was to offer the workingman an ordered, educational, self-improving alternative to the attractions of the tavern and the gaming house. This was, of course, an uphill battle, but it did produce some tangible results such as free museum admissions on holidays, and the passing of statutes that made it possible for municipalities to create a variety of public leisure institutions: libraries, museums, and parks. Although the physical realization of the ideal—public places of recreation accessible to all—took many years to achieve, the shift in perception was an important one. Leisure, previously a commercial affair, was becoming a public concern.

Another democratizing influence on nineteenth-century leisure, especially Sunday leisure, was train travel. Trains transported entertainers—whether circus performers or theater troupes—more quickly and conveniently than before, and provincial audiences could now enjoy almost the same quality of entertainment as metropolitan ones. More important, as the cost of travel came down, more people could afford to go farther for a spectacle. This ensured the growth of large recreational enterprises such as fairs and pleasure gardens, and of the major racecourses, which could now draw spectators of all classes from a considerable distance. It's important to note that, as Cunningham points out, during the nineteenth century "working people used the trains not to get to work, but to travel for pleasure." When the Crystal

Palace was reerected at Sydenham, in 1854, it was reached from London by rail, and the idea of taking the train for "a day in the country" caught on. Railway companies made concerted efforts to attract the public by reducing fares on holidays and by organizing Sunday excursions not only to fairs and racecourses but also to the seaside. Previously exclusive resorts such as Brighton and Blackpool began to fill with crowds of day-trippers.

Georgian leisure had always been an antidote to work—it removed the participant from the humdrum, everyday world of the workshop and placed him in the exciting atmosphere of sport and public spectacle. Thanks to the railways, this dislocation became literal, taking the Victorian factory worker out of the confines of the industrial city and into more congenial surroundings.

The immense changes that Sunday—and leisure—had undergone by the last quarter of the nineteenth century were admirably depicted by Seurat in *Grande Jatte*. The wooded island, a short train ride from the Gare Saint-Lazare, offered precisely the amenities that attracted the Sunday crowd: fresh air and verdure, opportunities for boating, fishing, and picnicking—an escape from the center of Paris, which, like London, was increasingly congested and crowded. Most homes were cramped, dreary, poorly lit and ill-ventilated. The city was an unhealthy place; until the turn of the century, outbreaks of typhoid, cholera, and smallpox were common in Paris. Little wonder that most people looked forward to getting away, even if only for a day.

What did they do on their outings? At first glance, most of the figures in *Grande Jatte* do not appear to be doing anything except strolling. The nineteenth century took the idea of "a walk in the park" seriously. Walking was physically healthful, and walking surrounded by nature was held to be spiritually uplifting—thus the growing popularity of mountain climbing and hiking. The first public parks were intended only for walking and contained no other facilities; they were deliberately introduced as a "civilizing" alternative to other recreations. One Manchester writer approvingly observed that "on Sunday, instead of loitering in the fields, dog-fighting, playing at pitch-and-toss, or being in the beerhouse, they [the public] go to some of those parks." He added, "They are also induced to dress better."

The island of Grande Jatte was not a formally planned park, but it had much in common with such places. Certainly the promenading figures that Seurat observed were well dressed: gentlemen in frock coats and top hats, ladies with fancy bonnets and parasols, exhibiting the curious silhouette that came from wearing a bustle, which was then the height of chic. But among these fashion plates in their Sunday best are other figures, whose costumes suggest a lesser social pedigree: the two hatless young women sitting on the grass, for example, or the nanny with the child. On closer inspection this "bourgeois scene" is not that at all, for it also includes working-class participants such as the wet nurse and the conscript soldiers. Or the reclining man in the foreground, whose billed cap, sleeveless singlet, and clay pipe mark him as a factory hand. At the other end of the social spectrum are the yachtsmen and the team of rowers, indulging in gentlemanly pastimes that were restricted to the prosperous bourgeois.

The mixture of social classes demonstrated the extent to which the middle-class ideals of the rational recreation movement had come to dominate French Sunday leisure. This domination was not total, however, for Grande Jatte was not only a place for boaters and picnickers, it also offered commercial entertainments. The island was the site of several cafés and skittle alleys, and of a dance hall that had a slightly risqué reputation. These entertainments are not visible in the picture, but Seurat has alluded to them, in typically circumspect fashion.* The busty woman in the

---

* Seurat's origins were bourgeois, and he exhibited many of that class's characteristics: perseverance, sobriety, and reserve. Degas's nickname for him was "the notary."

106

foreground, accompanying the elegant boulevardier, has a monkey on a leash. Art historian Richard Thomson has suggested that Seurat was making a cunning visual pun, for in contemporary Parisian slang *singesse,* or female monkey, meant a prostitute. He also points out that the well-dressed female figure at the water's edge, anomalously holding a fishing pole, may be an allusion to a common French metaphor that referred to prostitutes as "fishing" for clients (the French words for "fishing" and for "sin" sound the same).

The presence of strumpets in the park is a reminder of an earlier time, when the only women who frequented dance halls, as well as other places of public leisure such as taverns, pleasure gardens, casinos, and even music halls, were assumed to be—and generally were—prostitutes. The proper place for proper women was the home—public leisure was exclusively a male domain. This began to change when sports and recreations became upper-class leisure activities. Then, too, the popular Sunday outing was a family affair. After the middle of the nineteenth century, the respectable recreations of the seaside—and of the park—could safely be indulged in by women of all classes, as Seurat's painting demonstrates.

It is a mixture of sexes and classes that has come to enjoy a Sunday afternoon in the park. Nevertheless—or maybe because of this democratic rubbing of shoulders—the individuals in this calm setting choose to ignore one another, and appear engrossed in private reverie. They are all together, yet apart. This was yet another nineteenth-century change. Public leisure ceased to be local, class-bound, and familiar, and became instead increasingly communal. In the process, it also became more impersonal, almost anonymous. Now one went *away* to rest, and on the beach, or in the park, one took one's leisure in the company of strangers.

five

Keeping Saint Monday

The Oxford English Dictionary finds the earliest recorded use of the word "weekend" in an 1879 issue of *Notes and queries,* an English magazine. "In Staffordshire, if a person leaves home at the end of his week's work on the Saturday afternoon to spend the evening of Saturday and the following Sunday with friends at a distance," the entry goes, "he is said to be spending his week-end at So-and-so." The quotation is obviously a definition, which suggests that the word had only recently come into use. It is also important to note that the "week's work" is described as ending on Saturday afternoon. It was precisely this early ending to the week that produced a holiday period of a day and a half—the first weekend. This innovation—and it was a uniquely British one—occurred in roughly the third quarter of the nineteenth century. To understand how and why the weekend appeared when it did, let's examine how the nature of free time changed during the previous hundred years.

Throughout the eighteenth century, the work-week ended on Saturday evening; Sunday was the weekly day off. The Reformation and, later, Puritanism had made Sunday the weekly holy day in an attempt to displace the saints' days and religious festivals of Catholicism. Although the taboo on work was more or less respected, the strictures of Sabbatarianism that prohibited merriment and levity on the Lord's Day were rejected by most Englishmen, who saw the holiday as a chance to drink, gamble, and generally have a good time.

Only one official weekly holiday did not necessarily mean that the life of the average British worker was one of unremitting toil. Far from it. Work was always interrupted to commemorate the annual feasts of Christmas, New Year, and Whitsuntide (the days following the seventh Sunday after Easter). These traditional holidays were universally observed, but the length of the breaks varied. Depending on local convention, work stopped for anywhere from a few days to two weeks. In addition to the religious holidays, villages and rural parishes observed their own annual festivals or "wakes." These celebratory rituals, which dated from medieval times, were mainly secular and involved sports, dancing, and other public amusements.

Towns had their own festivals, less bucolic than those of the countryside. Stamford, in Lincolnshire, celebrated a special holiday; each November 13th, thousands of men and boys gathered in the streets for bull running, an event reminiscent of the famous festival that still takes place in Pamplona. The British today deride the Spanish passion for bullfighting, but their sensibility in this regard is, at least culturally speaking, recent—the Stamford run ended with the bull's being pushed off a bridge into the river, and then fished out and killed. The Stamford run is famous because it lasted the longest (well into the nineteenth century), but similar runs took place in many English towns. In London, bull running involved workers and apprentices in the Spitalfields weaving trades, who merrily chased and goaded the animal, provided by a local butcher; the popular event persisted until 1826 and it took several violent police actions to stop it.

Annual festivals like the bull run were not the only days off. There were also communal holidays associated with special, occasional events such as prizefights, horse races, and other sporting competitions, as well as fairs, circuses, and traveling menageries. When one of these attractions arrived in a village or town, regular work more or less stopped while people flocked to gape and marvel at the exotic animals, equestrian acrobats, and assorted human freaks and oddities.

The idea of spontaneously closing up shop or leaving the workbench for the pursuit of pleasure strikes the modern reader as irresponsible, but for the eighteenth-century worker the line between work and play was blurred; work was engaged in with a certain amount of playfulness, and play was always given serious attention. Moreover, many recreational activities were directly linked to the workplace, since trade guilds often organized their own outings, had their own singing and drinking clubs and their own preferred taverns.

Eighteenth-century workers had, as Hugh Cunningham puts it, "a high preference for leisure, and for long periods of it." This preference was hardly something new; what *was* new was the ability, in prosperous Georgian England, of so many people to indulge it. For the first time in their lives, many workers earned more than survival wages. Now they had choices: they could buy goods or leisure. They could work more and earn more, or they could forgo the extra wages and enjoy more free time instead. Most chose the latter course. This was especially true for the highly paid skilled workers, who had the most economic freedom; but even general laborers, who were employed at day rates, had a choice in the matter. Many of these worked intensively, often for much more than the customary ten hours a day, and then quit to enjoy themselves until their money ran out.

Of course, the amount of regular free time varied according to local custom and the strength of each trade union. But many—too many—were left out. The poorest people, especially women and children, who were paid the lowest wages, did not share in the prosperity and were obliged to work continuous and unremitting days, often twelve to fourteen hours long. Sunday was their only opportunity for rest, and for some, who were obliged to work seven days a week, not even that break was available. But the occupation that offered the least chance for leisure had nothing to do with factory work—it was domestic service. Servants were at their masters' beck and call and had little time of their own. One afternoon a week was the typical maid's day off.

Whenever people had a choice in the matter, however, work was characterized by an irregular mixture of days on and days off, a pattern that the historian E. P. Thompson described as "alternate bouts of intense labor and of idleness." This irregularity was exacerbated by the way holidays were prolonged. The London bull run, for example, which traditionally took place on Easter Monday, was almost always extended to the following day; other runs began on Sunday and continued for one or two days thereafter. Village wakes followed a similar pattern. It was not unusual for sporting events, fairs, and other celebrations to last several days. Since Sunday was always the official holiday, it was usually the days following that were added on. This produced a regular custom of staying away from work on Monday, frequently also on Tuesday, and then working long hours at the end of the week to catch up. Among some trades, the Monday holiday achieved what amounted to an official status. Weavers and miners, for example, regularly took a holiday on the Monday after payday—which occurred weekly, or biweekly. This practice became so common that it was called "keeping Saint Monday."

The origin of the Saint Monday tradition is obscure. Like the seven-day week, it was a custom that spread rapidly, despite the fact that it lacked any official sanction, because it appealed to people. Like the week, it was an institution whose genesis was explained by legends and folktales. According to some, keeping Saint Monday originated among tailors, whose shops were generally closed on Mondays. According to another story, the custom began with cobblers, tradesmen who were not held in high esteem since they, unlike real shoemakers, had only enough skill to mend shoes.* These slow-witted fellows were supposed to have forgotten the exact date of the feast day of their patron, Saint Crispin; remembering only

---

* Hence something "cobbled together" is considered to be clumsily or poorly made.

that it occurred on a Monday, they celebrated each "Saint" Monday instead. It is a charming tale, though unlikely to be true, for the Monday tradition also existed in France, Belgium, Prussia, and Sweden. Its widespread observance suggests that it may have been a popular reaction against the loss of the cherished medieval saints' days, which had been eliminated by Reformation clerics in Protestant countries and by demanding employers in Catholic Europe.

Cobblers had a reputation as great tipplers—"cobbler's punch" was a cure for a hangover—and in some versions of the story they were said to have needed the Monday holiday to recover from their Sunday excesses. That part of the legend rings true, for the custom of keeping Saint Monday was undoubtedly linked to heavy drinking. The eighteenth century's propensity for heavy drinking has already been mentioned; if anything, the consumption of alcohol increased during the first half of the nineteenth century, and did not begin to decline until the early 1900s. Since binges rarely lasted only one day, those workers who chose to "do a lushington" found themselves unable to get to work on the Monday morning. Here is Benjamin Disraeli writing about the fictitious industrial town of Wodgate, in his novel *Sybil, or the Two Nations*: "The men seldom exceed four days of labour in the week. On Sunday the master workmen begin to drink; for the apprentices there is dog-fighting without stint. On the Monday and Tuesday the whole population is drunk."

The habit of keeping Saint Monday was not ancient—it probably started at the end of the eighteenth century. It was directly linked to industrialization, since it was a way for workers to redress the balance between their free time and the longer and longer workdays being demanded by factory owners. This improvised temporal device also allowed the worker to thumb his nose at authority and assert his traditional freedom to come and go from the workplace as he willed. Once the practice of keeping Saint Monday took hold, it was hard to dislodge. It was still common when Disraeli published his novel, in 1845, and it lasted for decades more. Thomas Wright's well-known book on the habits and customs of the working classes, which appeared in 1867, describes Saint Monday as "the most noticeable holiday, the most thoroughly self-made and characteristic of them all . . . that greatest of small holidays." Wright described himself as a journeyman engineer, that is, a mechanic, and his views are therefore those of someone who was not unsympathetic to his subject. On Monday, he wrote, "[the workers] are refreshed by the rest of the previous day; the money received on the Saturday is not all spent; and those among them who consign their best suits to the custody of the pawnbroker during the greatest part of each week are still in the possession of the suits which they have redeemed from limbo on Saturday night." Dressed in his Sunday clothes, with a few shillings in his pocket, the idle worker could go out on the town and enjoy himself. Not a small part of this enjoyment was meeting friends and fellow tradesmen who were engaged in the same recreation.

According to E. P. Thompson, Saint Monday was observed "almost universally wherever small-scale, domestic and outwork industries existed"; it was also common among factory workers. Saint Monday may have started as an individual preference for staying away from work—whether for relaxation, for recovering from drunkenness, or both—but its popularity during the 1850s and '60s was ensured by the enterprise of the leisure industry. During that period, most sporting events such as horse races and cricket matches took place on Mondays, since their organizers knew that many of their working-class customers would be prepared to take the day off. Saint Monday was not only a day for animal baiting and prizefighting, however. Since many public events were prohibited on the Sabbath, Monday became the chief occasion for secular recreations. Attendance at botanical gardens and museums soared on Monday, which was also the day that ordinary people went to the theater and the dance hall and when workingmen's social clubs held their weekly meetings.

Michael R. Marrus, a British historian, defines leisure as "a free activity which an individual engages in for his own purposes, whatever these may be." The implication is that not all free time should be considered as leisure time, and that what distinguishes leisure from other recreations is the element of *personal choice*. This exercise of individual choice became a reality for a significant number of people for the first time during the late eighteenth and early nineteenth centuries, partly as the result of prosperity, partly as work habits changed, and partly as leisure activities passed from the world of custom and tradition (which offered little real choice) to the commercial world of the marketplace.

Chesterton maintained that the truest form of leisure was the freedom to do nothing. This was precisely the choice that the worker who kept Saint Monday made. This involved not only taking a particular day off but also the idea that it was the individual who was the master of his—and, more rarely, her—leisure. Because of its association with personal liberty, Saint Monday is sometimes described as if it were a preindustrial custom, like Maypole dancing or the village wake. Although this description is chronologically inaccurate, it is true that the ability to exercise the personal freedom to do nothing reflected preindustrial mores and stood in sharp contrast to the late-Victorian attitude to work, which stressed discipline and regularity, promoted creative recreation, and was critical of inactivity and idleness.

Saint Monday was a reflection of old habits, but it was also a premonition of what was to come. The "small holiday" prepared the way for the weekend. First, because it accustomed people to the advantages of a regular weekly break that consisted of more than one day. Second, because it served to popularize a new type of recreational activity—travel for pleasure.

Until the coming of the railway in the 1830s, modes of travel had been basically unchanged since ancient times. Short distances were covered on foot; longer trips were undertaken on horseback (although only by young and fit males) or in a horse-drawn carriage. Both involved bad roads, mishaps, and, for a long time, the perils of highwaymen. By the early 1800s, the last was no longer a problem, but travel continued to be something undertaken out of necessity, rarely for amusement. In Jane Austen's *Emma*, Mr. Knightley frets about the "evils of the journey" that he and his family are about to undertake from London to Highbury, and about the "fatigues of his own horses and coachmen." The modern reader is surprised to discover that the journey is a distance of only sixteen miles. But sixteen miles, by coach, took almost four hours, and it would have been an exceedingly unpleasant and uncomfortable four hours, swaying and bumping over rutted, muddy country roads.* In the same novel Emma's father, Mr. Wood-house, has a horror of carriages and hardly ever travels—except on foot; Emma's sister visits Highbury from London, but she does so infrequently. Most houseguests in *Emma* stay at Highbury for at least a week or two, since the slowness and discomfort of coach travel makes shorter visits impractical.

The time involved, as well as the expense, ensured that travel was a luxury, if not exactly enjoyed by, then at least restricted to, the moneyed and leisured classes. But the railway and Saint Monday changed all that. According to Douglas A. Reid, a historian at the University of Birmingham in England, cheap railway excursions in that city began in the summer of 1841. The custom established itself quickly, and in 1846, twenty-two excursions (many organized by workers' clubs) took place; more than three quarters of them occurred on a Monday. The train furnished the workingman and his family with a rapid and cheap means of travel, and the weekday holiday provided an entire free day to indulge it. "Eight hours at the seaside for three-and-sixpence," announced a contemporary advertisement. The Sunday-to-Monday holi-

---

* *Emma* was written in 1816. It wasn't until the 1830s that metaled roads became common, at least between major cities, and coach travel, in turn, became somewhat more comfortable and more rapid. On a good road, with frequent change of horses, a coach could attain the unprecedented speed of ten miles per hour.

day also meant that people could leave on a trip one day and return the next. This was not called "spending a weekend," but it differed little from the later practice. It only remained to transpose the holiday from Monday to Saturday.

The energy of entrepreneurs, assisted by advertising, was an important influence not only on the diffusion and persistence of Saint Monday but on leisure in general. Hence a curious and apparently contradictory situation: not so much the commercialization of leisure as the discovery of leisure, thanks to commerce. Beginning in the eighteenth century with magazines, coffeehouses, and music rooms, and continuing throughout the nineteenth century, with professional sports and holiday travel, the modern idea of personal leisure emerged at the same time as the business of leisure. The first could not have happened without the second.

Saint Monday had many critics. Religious groups actively campaigned against the tradition which they saw as linked to the drinking and dissipation that, in their eyes, dishonored the Sabbath. They were joined by middle-class social reformers and by proponents of rational recreation, who also had an interest in altering Sunday behavior. They wanted their countrymen to adopt the so-called Continental Sunday, a day on which French and Germans of all classes mingled together in easy and decorous intimacy in promenades and pleasure gardens—the kind of civilized Sunday in the park that was depicted a little later by Seurat in *Grande Jatte*. These were the sorts of Sunday activities that were promoted by such improving societies as the newly founded Young Men's Christian Association, the Sons of Temperance, and especially by the P.S.A., or Pleasant Sunday Afternoon. For all these groups, Saint Monday, and the popular working-class entertainments of which it was an integral part, was an enemy.*

One of the organizations that played a role in the debate was the Metropolitan Early Closing Association, established in London in 1842. Its members, who were drawn almost exclusively from the middle class, were concerned with the labor conditions of shop assistants, whose workday lasted up to eighteen hours. At that time, shops generally stayed open until ten or eleven o'clock in the evening, and even later during the summer months; the Association lobbied for a six o'clock closing time. It organized meetings and public appeals, and in a short time, chapters sprang up in Manchester, Birmingham, Liverpool, and all the other major English cities. Eventually its demands were made on behalf not only of shop assistants but

---

* The religious reformers and the proponents of rational recreation were not always on the same side, however, for the latter called for Sunday museum openings and band concerts, which were anathema to the Sabbatarians.

also of clerical workers in offices and warehouses.

The aims of the Early Closing Association, as it came to be called, were humanitarian but also religious. Since Sunday was the only holiday for the hardworking clerks, they used it partly for sleeping in and partly for recreation—understandably, church attendance was not a high priority. The hope of the Association was that a less arduous week would encourage more participation in Sunday worship. In 1855, this led to the suggestion of a one o'clock closing time on Saturday, which left a half-holiday for household chores and social activities—an evening at the dance hall or the pub—and permitted Sunday to be used exclusively for prayer and sober recreations. Since shop assistants had no union, this change required the voluntary acquiescence of individual shop owners, whose reactions varied considerably from city to city. Some types of shops—booksellers, druggists, and clothiers—adopted the shorter hours more readily than others.

The Early Closing Association must be credited with introducing the idea of the half-Saturday to the general public, but it achieved few other victories during its more-than-fifty-year life. There were some inherent contradictions in its aims. The more other off-duty clerks used Saturday afternoon for shopping, the more the remaining shops were encouraged to stay open. There was also the drawback that the Association was a top-down movement—the organization was initiated by the wealthy, and actually involved few clerks or shopkeepers. It relied on moral suasion rather than industrial action, and never managed to develop a strong political base.

It's unlikely that the Saturday half-holiday would have spread so rapidly if it hadn't been for support of the factory owners. It was becoming apparent to them that it was expensive and inefficient to operate machinery, especially steam engines, on a stop-and-go schedule, and it was impossible to plan production properly—and profitably—when a good part of the workforce might at any time disappear, without notice, to participate in some local celebration. Absenteeism was endemic, but efforts to impose disciplinary measures—locking out employees who did not appear, substituting women workers—had been ineffective, so ineffective that many owners just gave up and used Monday to effect repairs and maintenance on their idle machinery.

Employers had little to gain in insisting on a six-day week of twelve-hour workdays if, on some days, so few workers showed up that the factory had to be shut down anyway. The proposal of the Early Closing Association for a Saturday half-holiday offered a way out, and it came to be supported by factory owners, who were prepared to trade a half-day holiday on Saturday for a commitment to regular attendance on the part of their employees. Half-Saturdays and shorter workdays became the pattern followed by all later labor negotiations, and by legislation governing the length of the workday.

There were historical precedents for the Saturday half-holiday, which had existed for some time among certain trades in Scotland and the north of England. For weavers who worked at home, for example, Saturday afternoon was "reckoning time"; their weekly production was brought in to be counted, which naturally resulted in a shorter workday. Early Saturday closings are reported among cotton workers as far back as 1816, and also among paper workers in Lancashire and in the west of Scotland. Textile workers traditionally stopped work early on Saturday—payday—although this practice had died out by the nineteenth century. It was revived by the Ten Hours Bill (1847), a law that regulated the length of the workday in the northern textile industry, legislating a return to the customary ten hours—from six in the morning until six at night, with two hours off for meals. At the same time, the Bill mandated a "short Saturday" of eight hours. Several years later, the Factory Act required that Saturday work cease even earlier, at two o'clock in the afternoon. Over the next twenty years this practice spread across England, and came to include builders, lace workers, and many other trades. In 1874 a law was passed that reduced the length of Saturday work for all large industries throughout the nation to six and a half hours.

In his essay on the decline of the Saint Monday tradition, Douglas A. Reid suggested that the achievement of the Saturday half-holiday also depended on the acquiescence of the workers themselves, for "men had to wish to be converted and unless they did evangelism was not bound to succeed." But why did they agree to the new schedule? Giving up a full Monday holiday in exchange for a half-Saturday was not exactly a bargain; one might also expect that there would have been opposition to the loss of personal freedom—no longer being able to choose when to work and when not to. Opposition there was, but it was not universal. Only the elite trades, skilled and better paid, earned enough to absent themselves from work at will, and many of these did resist the loss of Saint Monday, continuing to work irregular days. But many workers couldn't afford to take Monday or any other day off. For the poorly paid laborers who worked six long days a week, an additional half-day holiday was a welcome break—they had nothing to lose. For others, keeping Saint Monday became impractical as a result of child-labor laws, which limited the number of daily hours children could be made to work, and deprived the individual artisans, who relied on young assistants, of the option of working extra-long hours at the end of the week to make up for the lost production of Saint Monday.

But often, the choice of the better-paid trades to exchange their freedom for more regular employment was voluntary. Spending habits were changing, and the growth in consumer demand and acquisitiveness, and hence in the importance of saving money, resulted in a higher value's being placed on regular wages. The attraction of money was displacing the attraction of free time. Then, too, the gradual spread of middle-class values meant that there were many workers who were critical of the profligate Saint Monday tradition—the excessive drinking and gambling—and whose clubs and societies supported the idea of a more disciplined and progressive work schedule.

For the social reformers, the difference between a Saturday and a Monday holiday was crucial. In criticizing Saint Monday they were not just suggesting that leisure activities be shifted from one day to another—they were trying to alter the nature of those activities.

Attacked on all sides, the Saint Monday tradition suffered a decline—though not all at once and not everywhere at the same rate. The idea of a Monday holiday did persist in the Bank Holidays Act of 1871, which required that three of the four new official national holidays fall on a Monday.* A few trades, such as cutlers, printers, and potters, held fast to Saint Monday until the turn of the century; E. P. Thomp-

---

* This raised the total number of bank holidays to eight. Lest this appear magnanimous, it is worth noting that before the first Bank Holidays Act of 1834, banks were closed on certain saints' days and anniversaries—thirty-three days every year.

son tells of British coal miners' keeping Saint Monday as late as the 1960s, but that was unusual. Sometimes the old custom managed to coexist with the new. As late as 1874, the American consul in Sheffield wrote that "every Monday is so generally a holiday, that it has come to be called Saint Monday . . . And this holiday is, in thousands of instances, protracted through the next day, so that large numbers of the workmen, stopping work on Saturday noon, do not commence again until the following Wednesday." But on the whole such behavior, once so common, was becoming the exception. For more and more workers, the week was assuming its modern shape: regular workdays followed by a regular period of leisure.

It was in the 1870s that people began to speak of "week-ending" or "spending the week-end." The country houses of the wealthy were generally located in the Home Counties, in the vicinity of London, and were now easily reached by train. It became fashionable to go there on Friday afternoon and return to the city on Monday, and these house parties became an important feature of upper-class social life.* Weekend

---

* According to Ralph Dutton, the Victorian weekend was a backward step; whereas eighteenth-century country-house life had provided a leisurely setting for visiting poets, painters, and writers, who would stay one or two weeks, the emphasis of the abbreviated house party was on entertainment, not culture.

outings, often to the seashore, were also available to the lower classes, although their weekend was shorter, extending from Saturday afternoon until Sunday evening.

According to one contemporary observer, Thomas Wright, "that the Saturday half-holiday movement is one of the most practically beneficial that has ever been inaugurated with a view to the social improvement of 'the masses,' no one who is acquainted with its workings will for a moment doubt." He approvingly described a variety of activities that working people indulged in on the Saturday half-holiday. The afternoon began with a leisurely midday meal at home, and was often followed by a weekly bath in the neighborhood bathhouse, an important institution at a time when few homes had running water, and one that was common in British and North American cities until well into the twentieth century. The rest of the daytime hours might be spent reading the paper, working around the house, attending a club, or strolling around town window-shopping. Saturday afternoon became a customary time for park concerts, soccer games, rowing, and bicycling. And, of course, drinking in the local pub, for despite the hopes of the reformers and Evangelicals, drinking was still the main leisure pastime of the working classes, whether the holiday occurred on Saturday or on Monday.

Wright emphasized that the afternoon was usually brought to a close in time for five o'clock tea, to leave plenty of time for the chief entertainment of the week—Saturday night. This was the time for an outing to the theater; most people brought their own food and drink into the cheap seats in the gallery. The music hall, an important influence on the spread of Saturday night, began as an adjunct to taverns but emerged as an independent entity in the 1840s, and proceeded to dominate British entertainment for the next eighty years. Like American vaudeville, the music hall presented its working-class audience with variety entertainment, chiefly songs. One of these catches the spirit of the new holiday, and of a new ritual:

> *Sweet Saturday night,*
> *When your week's work is over,*
> *That's the evening you make a throng,*
> *Take your dear little girls along.*
> *Sweet Saturday night:*
> *But this hour is Monday morning—*
> *To work you must go*
> *Though longing, I know*
> *For next Saturday night.*

Michael R. Marrus provocatively suggested that "for the broad masses of Europeans, leisure became a reality only in the nineteenth century." This is a slight exaggeration, since many recreational habits were established a hundred years earlier, and the Saint Monday tradition was already a kind of improvised leisure. But it is true that the nineteenth century saw, for the first time, a conception of leisure that was markedly different from what had come before. This was not the elite leisure of the aristocracy and landed gentry, for whom recreations such as shooting and fox hunting had become an all-consuming way of life. Nor was it like the traditional mix of leisure and work of ordinary people. No longer were work and play interchanged at will, no longer did they occur in the same milieu; there was now a special time for leisure, as well as a special place. Neither play as work nor work as play, middle-class leisure, which eventually infiltrated and influenced all of society, involved something new: a strict demarcation of a temporal and a physical boundary between leisure and work. This boundary—exemplified by the weekend—more than anything else characterizes modern leisure.

six

A World of Weekends

In the United States, unlike in Britain, there was no formal Saint Monday custom to uphold or to oppose; still, the American workplace before the nineteenth century was marked by casual attendance. Monday absenteeism was not uncommon, and, as in England, "blue Mondays" were the result of heavy Sunday drinking. Gradually employers imposed discipline in the workplace, and their employees retaliated by demanding shorter hours in exchange for regular attendance. On the whole, they were successful. In 1830 the workday was more than twelve hours long; over the next fifty years the workday grew shorter, and by the turn of the century some people worked as little as nine hours a day. The Sunday holiday was far from universally observed, however, certainly less than in Europe. Many industries—steel, for instance—operated on a seven-day schedule.

It wasn't until after World War I that the early Saturday closing began to be common in America, although by 1900 there were Saturday half-holidays during the summer months. Their exact origin is unclear, though the connection between a shorter Saturday and outdoor recreations such as swimming, boating, and baseball is obvious. Then, too, most North Americans had much warmer summers to contend with than Europeans; in the absence of air-conditioning, the summer heat in factories crowded with workers and machinery was close to unbearable.

There's no way of knowing whether Americans were aware of the British custom of stopping work at one o'clock on Saturday. In any case, different forces were at work on this side of the Atlantic. There were church groups and middle-class reformist organizations similar to the Early Closing Association, but the Saturday half-holiday came about largely as a result of the demands of working people themselves.

The shorter workweek was an integral part of the general trade-union agitation for shorter hours—specifically an eight-hour workday—a movement that started in the 1860s, after the Civil War. Its slogan was "Eight Hours for Work, Eight Hours for Rest, and Eight Hours for What We Will"; it was a goal that would take a long time to achieve. The average length of the workday in 1850 was about eleven hours; by 1900, thanks to the efforts of the labor movement, it was down to about nine hours, and continued to decline for the next three decades.

So-called short Saturdays began with the Typographical Union, which represented workers in job printing and in the newspaper and book trades. The nature of the newspaper business—at least that end of it—did not necessitate long hours. Print compositors had to finish their work in the late afternoon so the newspaper could appear the following morning, and so these workers led the fight for shorter work hours. By 1907, following several major strikes, the eight-hour day was a reality. Or almost. Many workers chose to follow a long-standing custom in the book and job trade and work an extra three quarters of an hour each weekday so that they could stop at noon on Saturday. Later this practice was officially recognized in the union's insistence on a forty-four-hour week: eight hours a day, and only four on Saturday. Other trades made similar demands. As early as 1912, a thirteen-week strike by New York City furriers forced employers to accede to a Saturday half-holiday.

Many union members wondered whether a six-day week of shorter days wasn't preferable to longer days and half-Saturdays off. Nevertheless, as in England, the appeal of a full afternoon holiday that was linked to Sunday was strong, and the custom spread. And spread rapidly. According to Roy Rosenzweig's study of workers and leisure in Worcester, Massachusetts, by the early 1920s a "growing number of firms . . . required only a half day's work on Saturday." It was not only blue-collar workers who wanted early closing. By 1929, the American Federation of Labor, in its call for a reduction of hours for federal government employees, made the shorter week a primary demand, "inasmuch as private business has now generally adopted the Saturday half-holiday practice throughout the year." A famous 1934 social study of suburban leisure patterns in Westchester County, New York, describes the Saturday half-holiday as a "standard" feature of the workweek for the "gainfully employed."

The largest adult occupational group in Westchester was classified as "white-collar," which underlines the widespread observance of the half-holiday not only among the trades but among clerical workers. By the 1930s, most offices in New York City closed their doors at noon on Saturday. The popularity of the custom must be attributed to a general demand for more time off by all classes of workers. This extra leisure was given over to a variety of pastimes. In the Westchester study, more than ninety percent of the leisure time of the admittedly middle-class occupational groups was taken up by seven types of activities: eating, visiting friends, reading, listening to the radio, sports, motoring for pleasure, and various types of public entertainment—a mixture of old and new. The first four activities could be enjoyed after work, during the week, but Saturday afternoons were for outdoor sports such as tennis and golf, and for pastimes like motoring. The half-day holiday was also convenient for shopping, especially at a time when many states still had restrictions on Sunday store openings. There were many things to do on a Saturday afternoon, but one big advantage of the half-holiday was that it coincided with the emergence of an important leisure institution: Saturday night.

In Britain, the popularity of Saturday night was helped along by the music hall; in the United States and Canada, this role was taken by a different urban entertainment—the movie theater. Movies had arrived on the urban scene just after the turn of the century as full-fledged mass entertainment in the form of the nickelodeon—a half-hour film for a five-cent admission. The low price (a ticket to a Broadway play cost more than a dollar) and the short duration gave it the appeal of fast-food restaurants today. People could drop in to see a one-reel melodrama or a slapstick comedy during their lunch break, after work, or, despite the protestation of religious groups, on Sunday, when many nickelodeons stayed open illegally. Although the public entertainments of choice for working people were still the saloon and the dance hall, the number of nickelodeons grew quickly, and by 1908 daily movie attendance in New York City was estimated at two hundred thousand people.

What happened next was common in the history of leisure: when too many people had too much fun, someone eventually objected. Play is rarely "harmless," at least from society's point of view. The "letting go" that is a fundamental attribute of play is a letting go of everyday behavior, but also, sometimes, of everyday morality and social conventions. In his classic study of play, *Homo Ludens,* Johan Huizinga observed that since play is older and more original than civilization, it is fundamentally antithetical to it. This opposition becomes more evident the more evolved, and the more serious, civilization becomes, and periodically leads to conflict. Play is often the loser. This is what happened in the Middle Ages to the popular anticlerical festivals, many of which came to be banned by the church, and later to the bull runs. The nickelodeons met with the same fate.

In 1908 the mayor of New York closed all 550 movie houses and nickelodeons in the city. His action reflected the outrage that many felt toward the new form of public entertainment. Respectable people considered movies an affront and a challenge to establishment sensibilities, not only because of their lowbrow and sometimes racy subject matter, which flew in the face of middle-class values and morality, but also because they did not accord with middle-class conceptions of leisure. The American equivalent of the British rational recreation movement did not find anything edifying in the distinctly proletarian entertainments of the nickelodeon, which often ridiculed authority figures such as policemen and politicians. That movie houses were often linked to saloons did not endear them to social reformers, nor did their attractiveness to children—and single women—and their flaunting of Sunday-closing laws. There was also an undercurrent of racial prejudice in the crusade against movies, for the inexpensive nickelodeons were particularly popular with European immigrants—you didn't need to understand English to enjoy a silent movie (in any case, more than half the films were foreign: French, German, and Italian)—and many of the theater owners were Jewish.

The aim of what became a great reforming campaign was not to prohibit movies but to "clean them up." As a result of expensive licensing fees (which went from $25 to $500), stricter building requirements and regulations, and review boards that scrutinized—and censored—movies, the nickelodeon was transformed. Movies became respectable family entertainment, and in the process turned into a major industry. Not only did the audience grow to include the middle class, but the films themselves expanded into full-length dramas such as D. W. Griffith's celebrated *The Birth of a Nation,* released in 1915 and a huge box-office success.

Griffith's aspirations were artistic and polemical—his films have been described as both messages or warnings—but it was his economic achievements that impressed entrepreneurs, for *The Birth of a Nation* grossed over $13 million. With the establishment of a West Coast filmmaking industry, mainly by Jewish-European immigrants—Adolph Zukor, Louis B. Mayer, Carl Laemmle, William Fox, the Warner brothers—movies abandoned Griffith's reformist Protestant course and returned to their original roots: entertaining the public. "The public pays the money," said Samuel Goldwyn. "It wants to be entertained. That's all I know."

By the 1920s, going to the movies was the chief public amusement of Americans. More money was spent on movies than on any other recreation. In only a decade, New York City alone acquired eight hundred movie theaters; there were more movie houses in the United States than in all Europe. The "Big Eight" producers, who owned most of these theaters, turned out more than seven hundred movies a year, large extravagant creations featuring "stars" whose offscreen lives in the adroitly mythologized world of "Hollywood" were as important to their fans as their film performances.

The movie had evolved from fast food to a three-course meal, and it was a fancy spread. Nickelodeons were small, sleazy storefront operations, seating no more than three hundred; movie theaters, which were located along prominent streets rather than in lower-class neighborhoods, were usually more than three times larger. At first the buildings were designed in the classical style—like libraries, museums, and other civic buildings—which accurately reflected the cultural aspirations of the reformed cinema. Eventually this decor proved too sedate, and the movie theater was transformed into the movie palace. Luxury replaced propriety. Flashy lobbies and uniformed ushers greeted the moviegoer, and a full orchestra accompanied the film. Baroque, rococo, Moorish, and Chinese interiors provided a glittering and sumptuous setting for what had become a glamorous event.

The movie palace provided an experience of luxury and wealth. People dressed up to go to the movies, just as they did to go to a restaurant or club, for, as Lary May astutely observes in his history of the early period of the motion picture industry, theater owners had consciously begun to associate moviegoing with nightlife. The brightly lit marquee, the chandeliers, the increasingly opulent interiors, and the spectacle of "opening night" all contributed to this effect.

More elaborate movies cost more to make, and admission prices rose accordingly. Higher ticket prices didn't discourage the public—quite the opposite, they raised the status of movies as entertainment. And since films were much longer, one no longer dropped in on a whim. Going to the movies now involved a "night out," for both women and men of all classes and ages. Frequently women and men together; movies were explicitly romantic, and so was going to the movies. Especially on Saturday night, since, for many people, Sunday was still a taboo day for courting. As for weekday evenings, not everyone felt like playing after a full day's work. The Saturday half-holiday, which left an early evening available for leisure activities, neatly coincided with the phenomenal popularity of moviegoing. Although movies and weekends developed independently, they reinforced each other. Movies were the main form of urban recreation, and Saturday night became the chief occasion for this celluloid excursion.

In Britain, the half-Saturday holiday emerged in the 1870s, and took sixty years to expand to a full day off. The American half-holiday appeared in the 1920s, and its expansion was, if anything, more rapid. Often, the weekend arrived in its full, two-day configuration. The first factory to adopt a five-day week was a New England spinning mill, in 1908, specifically to accommodate its Jewish workers. The six-day week had always made it hard for Orthodox Jews to observe the Sabbath, for if they took Saturday off and worked on Sunday, they risked offending the Christian majority. Moreover, as work patterns became increasingly standardized through union agreements, many Jews did not even have a choice, which threatened the

Sabbath tradition. The five-day week—in which both Saturday and Sunday were holidays—offered a convenient way out, and it came to be supported by Jewish workers, rabbis, community leaders, and some Jewish employers. In 1929, the Amalgamated Clothing Workers of America, composed largely of Jewish workers, became the first union to propose a five-day week.

At first the five-day week was common in only three industries: the (predominantly Jewish) needle trade, building construction (where well-organized unions had been aggressive in seeking shorter hours), and, to a lesser degree, printing and publishing, where the change from the half-Saturday to a full holiday was slower in coming. There were a few isolated cases of employers who voluntarily adopted the five-day week. The earliest and most notable of these was, curiously enough, Henry Ford, a staunch anti-unionist. In 1914, Ford reduced the daily hours in his plant from nine to eight; in 1926 he announced that henceforth his factories would also be closed all day Saturday. His rationale was that an increase in leisure time would support an increase in consumer spending, not the least on automobile travel and automobiles. This was a prescient view, for the weekend did eventually become associated with outings and pleasure trips. But in 1926, that was still in the future, and Ford was alone among businessmen in espousing the weekend. He was roundly criticized by both the National Industry Council and the National Association of Manufacturers.

The idea of a five-day week was denounced as not only uneconomic but irreligious. A 1926 newspaper cartoon by "Ding" Darling, who drew for the *New York Herald Tribune* and the *Des Moines Register,* captured the mood of the time. He depicted an overalled worker, representing the American Federation of Labor, sitting next to a pile of stone tablets—the Ten Commandments. One tablet, the Fourth Commandment, was cracked in two, and, as a horrified Moses looked on, the worker was enthusiastically carving a new one. The new inscription read: "5 days shalt thou labor and do all thy work, but the sixth & seventh days are your own to do anything you darn please." Darling pointedly included the hood of a Model T in one corner of the drawing.

In the end, what finally consolidated the two-day weekend was not altruism or activism or, paradoxically, prosperity; it was the Great Depression of 1929. Shorter hours came to be widely regarded as a remedy for unemployment—people would work less, but more people would have jobs. In 1932, the Goodyear Tire & Rubber Company of Akron, Ohio, instituted a thirty-six-hour week—six-hour shifts, six days a week. This arrangement, which became standard for many rubber workers, remained in force for several decades. Six-day weeks were unusual, however; most industries adopted a combination of shorter days and a five-day work schedule. Eventually New Deal legislation embodied in the Fair Labor Standards Act of 1938 mandated a maximum forty-hour week, although it was mute about the length of the workday. In 1940 the eight-hour day was written into law. The five-day week had arrived. Wartime production caused the workday to be lengthened to ten hours during the 1940s. This was temporary, however, and during the postwar period, as the economy returned to normal, the workday shortened again and finally stabilized at about eight hours.

Benjamin Hunnicutt, a sociologist at the University of Iowa, characterizes the period between 1920 and 1940 as one during which the movement for shorter hours faltered, and ended. That is true, but although the length of the workweek in 1949 was not much different than it had been in 1929, the shape of the week had been altered dramatically. After World War II, people weren't willing to return to a six- or even five-and-half-day week—they had become used to the five-and-two rhythm. The five-day week, and the two-day weekend, were now a fixture of American life.

Like the planetary week, the idea of the weekend emigrated from place to place and adapted to different

144

circumstances. And like the planetary week, the weekend spread quickly. The Early Closing Association put forward the idea of a short Saturday in 1855; a hundred years later, the two-day weekend was routine in Britain and America, and short Saturdays were common in most European countries, which adopted the full weekend ten or twenty years later. A 1979 study of leisure in the European Community found a remarkable consistency in the length of the workweek. According to a survey of collective agreements, no country exceeded a forty-hour week (in West Germany and Belgium the workweek was even shorter), and all countries observed the weekend.* But this consistency is deceiving, for the weekend arrived in each country in a different way.

In most places it's impossible to date the arrival of the weekend with any accuracy. This is not the case in Italy, where the weekend arrived precisely on June 20, 1935. Twelve years earlier, less than six months after the coup d'état that brought Mussolini to power, the Fascist government passed a bill that for the first time limited the length of the workday, to eight hours; the workweek continued at six days, its mandatory maximum length since 1907. In 1935, taking its cue from the Early Closing Association, the

---

* This despite a great variety in the length of annual paid holidays in different countries: in 1979 they ranged from a low of three weeks (Ireland) to as long as six weeks (West Germany); in Denmark, the *minimum* legal holiday was five weeks.

regime passed a nationwide law that established the *sabato fascista* and declared that henceforth the work-week would end at one o'clock on Saturday.

The Fascist weekend was a state institution. The government promoted a host of *dopolavoro* ("after-work") organizations to see to it that the new leisure was not squandered in the "banal imitation of bourgeois vices." There were special Saturday matinee performances of the opera (*sabato teatrale*) at greatly reduced prices, limited, by government directive, to low-income workers and pensioners. Saturday afternoon and Sunday were also occasions for special trains that took the masses on excursions to the countryside and the beach. Sports and outdoor activities were emphasized; when it came to leisure, the Fascists, like the Early Closers, were social reformers whose goal was to provide not merely free time but the right kind of free time.

Despite these attempts, the weekend asserted its individual character. Traditional pastimes—card playing, dominoes, American movies—remained popular. The languid game of *bocce,* denounced at first as lacking in manly vigor, proved resistant to reform, and was finally declared a national sport. Attempts to invent a new sport, called *volata,* which was to be an indigenous version of English soccer, failed. The *dopolavoro* proved more successful at appropriating traditional forms of play than at creating new ones. In

146

her fascinating study of leisure in Fascist Italy, Victoria de Grazia concludes that "there does indeed appear to be much that was not specifically 'fascist' about the regime's organization of leisure-time activities."

During the 1930s, state organizations similar to the *dopolavoro* were instituted in other European right-wing dictatorships: Salazar's Portugal, Franco's Spain, and Metaxas's Greece. The model for all these efforts was Nazi Germany. Immediately after coming to power in 1933, the German National Socialist government took several measures to combat unemployment: expanding the military, instituting a compulsory six-month labor service for young men, and encouraging women to leave the workforce. As in America, the length of the workweek was reduced drastically; anyone working twenty-four hours a week or more was ineligible for social benefits. Unions were abolished and replaced by the Labor Front under the direction of Dr. Robert Ley, who was also given the responsibility for the *Gleichschaltung* ("bringing into line") of free time.

Ley founded the *Kraft durch Freude* ("Strength through Joy"), a state organization that co-opted existing sports and hobby clubs, provided cheap tickets to the theater, opera, and concerts (there was a traveling KdF symphony orchestra), and instituted cheap, collective holiday travel for workers. Ley established special seaside and ski resorts, yachting and riding

147

schools, and even operated a fleet of ten cruise ships that sailed the Baltic and the Mediterranean. Thanks to such initiatives, one German worker in three was able to take part in some sort of vacation travel. Between 1932 and 1938, tourism doubled.

Unlike in Italy, there was no official sanction of the weekend; the emphasis of KdF was on holidays of one to two weeks. This is not surprising, since the Nazi conception of leisure, although it has been described as bourgeois, was really collective and not individual—hence the promotion of tourism rather than domestic relaxation. Even so, the weekend might have infiltrated the Third Reich had a famous project reached fruition. In 1938, the Labor Front was put in charge of building the Volkswagen—Hitler's brainchild, lifted from Henry Ford—also known as the KdF car. This inexpensive automobile would take workers and their families on short jaunts over the newly constructed autobahns. But preparations for war brought an end both to the Nazi car and to the nascent Nazi weekend. By 1936 there were labor shortages, and official reductions to the workweek had ceased; by 1938 factories were working overtime producing war matériel, the workweek was up to more than forty-seven hours, and the KdF car was transformed into a military vehicle.

The weekend finally arrived to Germany after the war; in France developments were equally slow.

During the 1880s, when more and more British workers had Saturday afternoon off, the French working
people depicted in Seurat's painting still had only Sunday as a weekly holiday—on Saturday the island of
Grande Jatte would have been empty, except for some
middle-class boaters. Even Sunday was not a compulsory holiday; not until the early 1900s was legislation passed limiting the length of the workweek to
six days. As for the workday, it was set at a long
twelve hours. It was only after World War I that the
eight-hour workday was introduced, and it was
longer still before the Saturday half-holiday arrived.
When it did, in recognition of its origin, the new five-
and-a-half-day work schedule became known as *la
semaine anglaise*—"the English week."

There were attempts to introduce a universal five-
day week by the Popular Front government in 1936,
but these were curtailed by the demands of defense
production. Most French workers worked six days a
week; some, if they were lucky, had Saturday morning off. The English week lasted fifty years; as late as
1965, the French workweek was still five and a half
days, and averaged forty-six hours. In 1968, however,
it was reduced, and, over the next decade, the workweek fell to forty-one hours, chiefly as a result of the
arrival of the two-day weekend.

The two-day weekend was taken up belatedly but
with enthusiasm. Not that leisure time was lacking

in France. Unlike in England, where the weekend preceded the vacation, in France the middle class had been taking long summer holidays at seaside resorts, health spas, and Alpine hostelries, which were easily accessible by railway, since the turn of the century. The summer vacation traditionally lasted the entire month of August and had an importance unknown in English-speaking countries. Nevertheless, the appeal of a regular weekly break was strong. In France, as in America, the shorter workweek resulted from a combination of labor union demands, economic prosperity, and individual car ownership. The influence of the latter should not be underestimated. Automobile touring had long been popular in France—Michelin began publishing its guides in 1900—but had been restricted to the wealthy. Between 1950 and 1965, car ownership jumped from ten percent of all French households to fifty, vastly increasing the popularity of short weekend excursions.*

One society that showed reluctance to adopt the weekend was Israel, despite the fact that the Jews could claim to have invented the seventh-day leisure

---

* By 1967 weekend automobile traffic—and the accompanying carnage on the highway—was enough of a French fact of life to be savagely parodied by Jean-Luc Godard in a film titled *Weekend*.

break, and despite the fact that Israel was a country that adopted many Western institutions. In the new state of Israel, in 1948, the Sabbath was the only weekly holiday, prescribed by both religion and cultural tradition. For a long time there was little interest from either legislators or labor unions in shortening the workweek. This probably resulted from the economic pressures of building a country from scratch and the prevailing and necessary pioneer work ethic. Israelis also feared that increasing consumption on recreation might fuel inflation, and that an extra day of leisure might in some way devalue the Sabbath. Interestingly, Orthodox Jews, who were a significant minority, supported the establishment of the weekend; like the British Early Closers, they hoped that a second day of rest might provide an outlet for the sort of profane activities that, they felt, dishonored the Sabbath.

A 1970 survey found that fully two thirds of the Israeli population were in favor of a five-day week, and its authors took this as firm evidence that "sooner or later the five-day week will come." It's been a slow process. Today, the weekend is still far from universally observed in Israel, although it is making headway. The army still operates on a six-day schedule, and so do schools; only in the last five years have major enterprises begun to give their employees the weekend (Friday and Saturday) off. But the weekend is already having a major impact on Israeli life: weekend driving has increased, as have recreations such as camping and skiing.

Many of Israel's first immigrants came from Russia and Poland, where most people worked six days a week. In prewar Poland the half-day Saturday holiday did exist—it was known as "English Saturday"—but it was generally restricted to management. The Communist regime continued the custom, fixing the official workweek at six days of eight hours each. During the 1970s, one and then two free Saturdays a month were gradually introduced by certain industries, although these were not really holidays, since the extra time off had to be made up during the week.

This situation changed radically after the Solidarity strikes that began in the Lenin Shipyard in August 1980. A key demand of the strikers was for "free Saturdays without the need to work them off later," which became a clause of the famous Gdansk Agreement between Solidarity and the government. A few months later, in January 1981, the government announced it would be impossible to implement free Saturdays, owing to the worsening state of the national economy. This statement enraged the workers, and wildcat strikes broke out in many towns. Feelings were so strong on the issue that even Solidarity's charismatic leader, Lech Walesa, was unable to convince his membership to return to work. A last-minute compromise (three free Saturdays a month) averted a general strike that probably would have resulted in the declaration of a state of emergency and possibly even Soviet military intervention.

The turmoil over free Saturdays did have one less happy consequence—as a result of the civil disturbances and the evident weakness of the regime, an army man, General Jaruzelski, was appointed prime minister. By the end of the year the general had launched a military coup, instituted martial law, and brought Solidarity to a (temporary) end. The reforms to the workweek remained, however, and the weekend became a part of everyday Polish life.

A survey of Polish leisure habits in the years 1976 to 1984 shows that this extra free time was not used exclusively for leisure, since many people worked overtime or took second jobs. Saturdays were also an opportunity for shopping, a time-consuming activity involving long shop lines and hours spent seeking out black-market opportunities. If they were not working or shopping, most Poles spent the weekend at home. A lack of money meant that they could afford only those leisure activities that could be done cheaply, such as chatting with friends, reading, inexpensive hobbies, listening to the radio, and watching television. Only two types of free-time activities seem to have been widely practiced outside the house: going for walks and going to church.

The types of entertainments (movies, theater, restaurants, sporting events) that served to promote the
weekend in prosperous societies were unavailable to
most Poles, and actually declined in importance during the 1980s. So did participation in leisure activities
that required expensive equipment (tennis, boating)
or travel (skiing, hiking). Although car ownership
started to rise in the early 1970s, gas rationing discouraged holiday travel, and for most people, even
public transportation was too expensive. The result
was that the weekend excursions so closely associated
with the two-day holiday in Britain, America, and
France played only a minor role in the development
of the Polish weekend.

In 1980, when Solidarity members demanded
more free time on weekends, there were no entrepreneurs serving up a smorgasbord of leisure activities for the two-day break, no railway companies
promoting weekend destinations, no saloons or dance
halls. What there was—what is always a component
of the weekend, even if it's sometimes hidden
under layers of glossy diversions—was the promise
of personal freedom. The limited number of leisure
activities available, or affordable, was undoubtedly a
frustration for some—"doing nothing" quickly loses
its appeal when it is imposed and not freely chosen—
but the lure of time for oneself was as strong in Poland
as anywhere else. If Polish workers couldn't do "any-

thing they darn pleased" on the sixth and seventh days, they could at least do some things, which was attraction enough.

The absence of commercial blandishments in the chaste Polish weekend is unusual. It contradicts the general tendency of the weekend to arrive in societies at moments of prosperity, when a wide range of entertainments and recreations is becoming available to people who, in turn, want a regular weekly break to pursue them. But even more unusual is the relationship between the weekend and the people with the highest per capita income in the world—the Japanese.

Industrialization came late to Japan, and the country lagged behind others in its work legislation. It wasn't until 1926, for example, that a law was passed limiting the length of the workday for women and young children, and even so, it was set at eleven hours and allowed fifteen-hour days under certain circumstances. In 1939, when the eight-hour day and the five-day week were already common in the United States, the average Japanese worked more than ten hours a day, six days a week. The traditional values of Japanese society stressed conformity and discipline—no absenteeism or Saint Mondays here, and no confrontational unions to demand more free time.

The six-day week persisted throughout the difficult postwar reconstruction period, which was to be expected. But even during the 1960s and 1970s, when an increasingly wealthy society might have relaxed, there was no easing of this hardworking schedule. In 1978, the average Japanese outworked the average American by more than 200 hours a year. That same year, Herman Kahn published *The Japanese Challenge*, in which he observed that although Japan lagged behind other industrial countries in reducing the length of the workweek, he expected the current prosperity to soon produce a great increase in the availability of leisure time. "As Japan gets richer," he wrote, "like other affluent countries, it will almost inevitably pay more attention to welfare, consumption, and leisure."

Kahn was right about the first priority, partly right about the second, but wrong about the third. A decade later, most Japanese still work eight- and nine-hour days, Monday to Saturday. A few Japanese companies—about six percent, or about twenty-eight percent of employees nationwide—have instituted a five-day workweek, but this figure is deceptive since many people work on Saturdays for the overtime.

And the lack of weekends is not compensated by long vacations. Although Japanese law requires annual paid holidays of between six and twenty days, these are irregularly observed. According to sociologist Ezra F. Vogel, the typical salaried worker is hesitant to take all the free time to which he is entitled:

"If he were to request his full vacation time, he would be regarded as selfish and disloyal by his co-workers and by his superiors." Others have suggested that the Japanese are simply too absorbed in their work to take vacations. Whether it is caused by social pressure or personal choice, the result is the same—except for the so-called Golden Week, a period in early May when several national holidays in a row give everyone a four- or five-day break, many Japanese never have a vacation.

The most common explanation for this national reluctance to relax is that the Japanese are drones who prefer work to play. Certainly they seem to have an impressive capacity for hard work, which is generally felt to be the chief ingredient in the country's economic success. This attitude to work begins early. Children attend school on Saturday morning, and most take extra night classes. Summer school vacations are short, a month shorter than in America. Opinion polls regularly show that "being a hard worker" rates high among people's aspirations. Some sociologists have made a case for the existence of a "Protestant ethic" in Japan, although most of the population is not religious. There are, indeed, many parallels between modern Japan and the nineteenth-century industrial revolution, but one obvious difference: it was Protestant Britain and America that pioneered the weekend.

It's true that the Japanese language has no word for "leisure" and uses the English equivalent (just as it has adopted the French *vacances* for "holidays"), but the suggestion that the Japanese are not interested in play is contradicted by the extremely wide variety of commercial recreational activities available to them. Most popular sports, like baseball and golf, are recent imports from abroad, but adult comic books (*manga*), which go back to the beginning of the eighteenth century and are now a huge industry, are uniquely Japanese. So is *pachinko,* a sort of vertical pinball that is played for money and is as ubiquitous in Japan as lottery tickets are in France. It's also worth recalling that Japan is the home of the Walkman, the home video camera, Nintendo, and a host of electronic gadgets intended specifically for leisure.

The average Japanese family has increased its spending on leisure activities eightfold since 1965. But unlike Poles, who had free time, but empty shelves, the Japanese have to work long and hard to take advantage of the array of consumer goods—much longer and harder than Americans. According to James Fallows, a journalist who has written extensively on the Far East, restrictive trade tariffs and cartel-based prices mean that Japanese consumers pay almost twice as much as Americans for the same products. Put another way, high prices at home support low prices abroad. When the high cost of consumer goods is coupled with the cost of food and housing, abnormally high (by European and American standards), the Japanese propensity for putting in overtime at the office and factory makes more sense.

While the Japanese enjoy much less free time than European and American workers, there is also a difference in the role of leisure in their lives. In contemporary Western societies leisure has become an antidote to work; there are physical and temporal distinctions between the two. In Japan the line between work and leisure is often blurred, especially for salarymen—white-collar workers in large corporations. Eating and drinking after work are often done at company expense, and much free time in the evening is spent in the company of one's workmates. In some ways this situation is like the one in eighteenth-century Britain, when workers engaged in drinking, sports, and games not with families or friends but with fellow tradesmen and guild members.

Observers of Japanese daily life suggest another reason for long hours at the office: the Japanese workplace is invariably larger and more comfortable than the home. Japanese housing is cramped and notoriously lacking in amenities, despite its high cost. According to a recent survey, the top five leisure activities in 1984, 1985, and 1986 were dining out, driving, domestic travel, drinking (out), and going to the zoo, botanical garden, aquarium, or museum—all pastimes that take place outside the home.

In Poland the weekend was almost completely a

domestic institution. Even in Europe and America, where there were plenty of public entertainments, and possibilities for weekend travel, the evolution of the weekend was linked to the growing importance of home-life. Saturday night out was an important tradition, and so was going for a Sunday outing or drive, but people spent most of their free time at home. Maybe the weekend's lack of popularity in Japan can be explained in part by the inadequacies of the Japanese home. After all, most of us spend at least a good part of our weekends relaxing at home— still the best place to "do nothing"—and if one's home is poorly heated, noisy, uncomfortable, and crowded, the pleasures of the weekend are considerably diminished.

Old habits die hard, but the Japanese may still get the weekend whether they like it or not. In April 1990, the Japanese government signed a trade agreement with the United States that included, among other things, a promise to shorten the workweek for its employees to five days and to encourage private companies to do the same. This "vow of future sloth," as one sarcastic American editorialist called it, reflects an attempt by American trade negotiators to narrow the trade gap between the two nations by demanding that the Japanese work less hard—or at least less long. It's unlikely that a shorter workweek will restrain the productive Japanese economy, but it will be interesting to see what effect it will have on Japanese everyday life. It will likely be different than elsewhere. After all, the weekend has traditionally been considered a reward; this is the first time it will be imposed as a punishment.

seven

Retreats

Several miles from my house, beside the road I take to drive to the village, I pass what is locally known as a *terrain de camping;* one of several such installations in the vicinity. The other campgrounds are identified by colorful roadside billboards with evocative names like Coolbreeze and Acapulco, but this one, inexplicably, is named Canne de Bois, or "the wooden walking stick." This makes it sound like a refuge for the elderly, but its occupants are mainly families with children. It's also inaccurate to describe it as a campground, for there are no tents here. When it opened, forty-five years ago, Canne de Bois did provide space for campers. Today, instead of temporary canvas shelters, there are dozens of small cabins and permanently parked house trailers, not shiny Airstreams but small, weathered caravans that haven't seen the open road for decades. Mixed among them are newer recreational vehicles, a few mobile homes, and even two or three small houses, perched precariously on piers of cement blocks. This motley architectural collection is located partly in open ground and partly among trees, around the edges of a man-made pond.

Despite its attractive natural setting, the general appearance of Canne de Bois is not exactly pretty. The house trailers are shrouded in a carapace of verandas, screened porches, lean-tos, and other homemade additions that attest to years of gradual and fragmentary accretion. It doesn't help that the building materials are flimsy and inexpensive—metal sheeting and painted plywood—or that the workmanship is slapdash. There's an atmosphere of impermanence—everything appears to be awaiting completion or to have been left unfinished. What little space there is on the tiny plots, which are surrounded by low fences and hedges, is crowded with an assortment of garden furniture, picnic tables, swings, concrete patios, decks, prefabricated garden sheds, barbecues, and lawn ornaments. The narrow, unpaved roads that snake around the settlement have streetlights and even street names, but this attempt at urbanity only accentuates the makeshift character of the whole.

Although Canne de Bois consists of individual homes on individual plots of land, its heterogeneity makes it unlike any suburban development I have ever seen. Nor does it exhibit the contrived picturesqueness of a Club Med. Instead, it reminds me of the shantytowns that I've visited on the fringes of cities in the Third World. This comparison is not intended critically. What these gritty, do-it-yourself neighborhoods lack in urbanity and visual coherence they make up in a liveliness that mirrors the resourcefulness of the occupant-builders, who are struggling to make a place for themselves with extremely modest means. The same spirit of individual enterprise and ambition is evident in the improvised homes of the Quebec campground.

The similarity between shantytowns and campgrounds was noticed first by the Dutch architect John Habraken, who observed that in both types of settlements the emphasis was on the unfettered creation of private and family spaces, while the public and communal domain was secondary and consisted of whatever was left over. This, Habraken pointed out, was almost exactly the reverse of what happens in most planned housing developments, where opportunities for personal choice are severely limited and the individual householder is required by zoning ordinances, building regulations, and other rules to adjust himself—and his dwelling—to the needs of the community.

Canne de Bois differs in another important respect from most conventional communities. Throughout the long Canadian winter the house trailers and cabins are empty and blanketed in snow, the pond is frozen over, and the bare trees reveal the surprising spread of the settlement, which extends more than half a mile from the highway. After the spring, which comes suddenly and offers a brief transition to full-blown summer weather, the "campers" appear. They remove the plywood sheets that cover the windows, fill up their propane tanks, and take the lawn furniture out of storage. The spaces in front of the homes sprout awnings and colorful umbrellas; the access road fills up with cars, and the pond fills up with swimmers and pedal boats. At night, street lamps and porch lights illuminate the previously dark space. Some people have attached strings of Christmas-tree lights to their homes, and the settlement takes on the festive air of an amusement park or pleasure garden.

From May until September, Canne de Bois accommodates 320 families, but these temporary residents make surprisingly little impression on the life of the village. Most arrive late on Friday night and leave on Sunday evening; in the interval, they generally stay in the campground. I sometimes see them in the supermarket on Saturday morning, buying cases of beer for the weekend, or in the convenience store picking up a newspaper. They are identifiable by their colorful attire and their Bermuda shorts and sandals—the local farmers favor green work clothes and baseball caps—and by their noisy behavior and lighthearted demeanor. One can hardly begrudge them their jollity—they are, after all, on holiday.

Just as altered dress and behavior distinguish the

weekenders from the permanent residents, the little cabins and caravans also have a distinctive character. Some plots are entered through a romantic trellised gateway, and the gardens contain many conventional symbols of rusticity—decorative fences, improvised gazebos, imitation wells. Lest there be any confusion about the meaning of these architectural elements, one camper has put up a hand-carved sign outside his modified caravan. *Royaume des biches,* it reads— "Kingdom of the Hinds."

The naming of country retreats has a long tradition. Almost two millennia ago, Pliny the Younger named his famous villa "Laurentum." Villa was a Latin word that the ancient Romans used to describe the country estates they maintained on the outskirts of their cities. There they would go in the summer to enjoy the cooler weather, and at other times of the year to savor the tranquil, pastoral atmosphere. Pliny, who lived in the first century A.D., devoted one of his many letters to a description of his own villa, in Latium, on the shore of the Tyrrhenian Sea not far from Ostia Antica, the port of Rome.

With becoming modesty Pliny described Laurentum as "large enough for my needs but not expensive to keep up." By modern standards, however, it was a large complex of buildings. Pliny was a successful lawyer and public administrator who at a young age was appointed consul, or chief magistrate, the highest bureaucratic post in the republic, and his villa reflected his status and wealth. The spread-out country house contained a gymnasium, a warmed swimming bath (with a view of the sea), a ball court, several public rooms, a banqueting hall as well as a dining room, apartments for himself and his guests, and slave quarters.

On one side of the compound was a terrace, "scented with violets," that overlooked the sea and was flanked by a covered arcade leading to a small building that contained Pliny's private suite. He was particularly fond of these rooms, since he had them built himself (one has the impression that the rest of the house was built by an earlier owner). "*Amores mei, revera amores,*" he wrote of them—"really and truly my favorites." This self-contained pavilion was divided into three rooms: a bedchamber, a *heliocaminus,* or sun-room (usually a roofless space, protected from the wind), and a sitting room, or, rather, reclining room, for the Romans used couches. From his couch Pliny could enjoy views on three sides: adjacent woods, neighboring villas, and the sea itself. Here, undisturbed by the bustle of his household, he could retire to read and write, or indulge, as he once wrote, in "that indolent but agreeable condition of doing nothing."

Of Pliny's villa there is no trace save the written record, but the environs of Rome are dotted with the ruins of such villas—that of Hadrian, at Tivoli, is the most famous. The practical Romans did not build their estates for pleasure alone; villas were usually the seats of large farms worked by tenant farmers whose rents were an important source of income for the wealthy landlords. Pliny himself, who would be reckoned a millionaire today, owned a large estate at Tifernum, in the present-day region of Umbria, about 150 miles north of Rome. But he described Laurentum, which had no farm, as his favorite country house. "For there," he wrote in another letter, "I do most of my writing, and, instead of the land I lack, I work to cultivate myself; so that I have a harvest in my desk to show you in place of full granaries elsewhere."

Laurentum was not surrounded, as most villas were, by fields and vineyards. Sitting on his terrace, Pliny gazed out not at his possessions but at the sea—ever the pragmatic Roman, he noted that it provided few fish of any value. When he went for a walk, it was not among his crops but on the beach. This made Laurentum an unusual villa, a thoroughly modern idea of a city dweller's refuge: unencumbered by practical function, quiet, relaxed, and natural.

By the time of the Renaissance, the distinction between farms and country retreats was explicit. The fifteenth-century architect Leon Battista Alberti devoted two chapters of his ten books on architecture to the subject of country houses. He differentiated between rural houses that were intended for farmers and villas for gentlemen; farmers, he suggested, required homes designed for utility, gentlemen for pleasure. Pleasure here included the rustic diversions of fishing and hunting, horseback riding, swimming, walking, reading, and "the delights of gardens"; in other words, exactly the pastimes that are still associated with a weekend in the country.

Neither the Florentine patrician that Alberti had in mind nor a Roman gentleman such as Pliny observed weekends, of course, but both would have used their villas more like weekend cottages than like vacation houses. Villas were generally built close to the city; in fact, the villa districts around Rome, such as Praeneste or Tusculum—where Cicero had a summer house—constituted the first suburbs. Laurentum was not one of these fashionable spots. It was slightly farther away from Rome—seventeen miles—but good roads made this a shorter and easier journey than that undertaken by Mr. Knightley in *Emma*. Pliny, who spent a good part of each summer at his Umbrian estate, traveled frequently to Laurentum during the winter. He described the trip as "rather heavy and slow-going if you drive [by carriage], but soft and easily covered on horseback," short enough that "it is possible to spend the night there after necessary business is done, without having cut short or hurried the day's work." In a similar vein, Alberti pointed out that "if the villa is not distant, but close by a gate of the city, it will make it easier and more convenient to flit, with wife and children, between town and villa, whenever desirable." Commuting to the cottage clearly has a long history.

The weekenders at Canne de Bois also visit their homemade villas regularly. They come from the city—that is, from Montreal, less than an hour away by car, a shorter trip than Pliny made to reach his villa. The pond replaces the emerald Tyrrhenian Sea, a horseshoe pitch the marble ball court, and an outdoor picnic table the banqueting hall. The gardens are decorated with cement birdbaths and fiberglass urns instead of with Hellenic statues. The environment is different, but the sentiment is similar. Indeed, the little cabins, although undoubtedly less elegant, are like Pliny's private pavilion—intimate, self-made, cozy little sanctuaries.

The chief difference is one of wealth. Like most working-class Montrealers, the inhabitants of Canne de Bois inhabit walk-up flats in the tall, narrow row houses that make up most of the city's housing and which give older Montreal neighborhoods the appearance of a nineteenth-century European town. Since most of these people are tenants, the caravans and cabins of Canne de Bois are not "second homes" but—in terms of ownership—first homes.* This is not unusual. The weekend cottage is frequently the only way people of modest means can own a home. Indeed, as urban housing prices soar to new, unapproachable levels, the weekend house may become, for many, the only real estate they will ever own. Rural land is inexpensive, and rudimentary rural building regulations—or their lack—allow the individual to build slowly, inexpertly, and hence cheaply. In that sense, a summer colony like Canne de Bois acquires greater significance than first meets the eye. What appear to be improvised "play" houses carry a sense of real seriousness, for although they are not inhabited continuously, for their owners, at least, they embody a sense of permanence and attachment.

The idea of having a "place in the country" probably entered human consciousness at the same time as people began living in cities. It was a reaction to the constraints of the rules and regulations that governed behavior in urban society, and was also a way to temporarily escape the curbs that city living inevitably put on the individual. In Italy villas continued to be built by patrician families throughout the Renaissance, often in the same places as their Roman

---

* The plots at Canne de Bois are rented, but the structures are privately owned. If a homeowner moves, the building is sold to another "tenant"; if the home has been enlarged or improved, the builder recoups his investment with a profit.

predecessors. Nor was the country house restricted to the upper classes. In 1598, when John Stow published *The Survey of London,* he remarked that people were erecting "summer-houses" surrounded by gardens just outside the city walls. These buildings probably belonged to merchants and wealthy shopkeepers.

Stow was critical of these summer houses, which were festooned with quaint turrets and fanciful chimneys, and he deplored their lack of any function save "show and pleasure." He had missed the point. These early versions of weekend cottages were not intended to be serious, and their freedom from architectural convention was not a sign of "the vanity of men's minds," as Stow maintained, but a reflection of their owners' temporary liberation. In these playful houses they had the freedom to behave as they liked, to do what they wanted and when they wanted. They could discard the uniformity of the city in architecture as they did in dress.*

The expressiveness and fantasy of the villa, or the summer cottage, are qualities not usually found in urban domestic buildings. Whether it's the gaily painted caravans of Canne de Bois or the extravagant log concoctions—euphemistically called "camps"—that William West Durant built for upper-class New

---

* Both Pliny and Alberti singled out informal dress as an advantage of villa life.

Yorkers in the Adirondacks, country retreats have always been an opportunity to break loose from the architectural constraints of the city.

Pliny loved the rustic surroundings of his villa and the simple life he led at Laurentum. The building itself, however, was as elegant as his city house, and contained all the comforts a sophisticated Roman could want. The idea of making the country retreat itself rustic grew out of the European Romantic movement, at the end of the eighteenth century. In architecture, as in painting and literature, Romanticism encouraged an awareness of the countryside and of traditional rural building styles. One consequence was the so-called *cottage orné* (ornamented cottage) that became fashionable in England during the Regency, and was the model for the holiday retreats of the middle class. Rambling, picturesque, and above all, rustic, the *cottage orné* provided an appropriate architectural image for anyone seeking an antidote to city living.

The search for the picturesque often led to a bizarre exoticism, and the villas of the wealthy took on more and more eccentric forms, forms that would have appalled Pliny: Swiss chalets, Norman keeps, medieval castles, Chinese pagodas, Gothic ruins, Moorish mosques, even Hindu palaces such as the Royal Pavilion at Brighton. The frankly fake rusticity of the *cottage orné* did not please Coleridge, for example, who ridiculed the "cottage of gentility" as a sign of "pride that apes humility." That sounds like Stow's complaint about the "vanity of men's minds." It is true that many of these cottages overdid it, with rough tree trunks supporting porch roofs and elaborate decors hidden under thatched roofs and behind cob walls.

Probably the first *cottage orné,* or rather *village orné,* was the famous hamlet built for Marie Antoinette at Versailles, in about 1781. A few years earlier, Louis XVI had given the queen the summer house of Petit Trianon, built by his father a decade before. Marie Antoinette surrounded the exquisite house with gardens in the fashionable "English" style, planted to resemble the natural landscape. She made twice-yearly "trips" to her retreat, in the spring and summer, to get away from the public life of the palace.

Petit Trianon was used like a summer cottage, but it was really a miniature château. Seeking something more natural—or, as Jean-Jacques Rousseau taught, seeking "to return to nature"—the queen had built nearby a mock-Norman village of romantic thatched cottages. Set in an lovely, naturalistic landscape, the charming structures, designed by the architect Richard Mique, included a mill, a dairy, and a dovecote. Despite their names, these buildings had purely recreational functions—they were for informal dining, billiards, backgammon, and dancing.

It's easy to make fun of a queen who pretends to be a country lass, eating ice cream off marble tables in the "dairy," picking flowers in the garden, or standing with a fishing pole at the edge of an artificial pond. But were her affectations really so different from what many modern city dwellers do on weekends: stockbrokers wearing old clothes and driving tractors, office workers in checked shirts chopping wood at the cottage, bus drivers putting on camouflage gear and going hunting, or pharmacists in sou'westers messing about in boats? Marie Antoinette's hamlet was a make-believe world, but so are all country retreats.

If I were to ask the inhabitants of Canne de Bois why they come here each weekend, they would answer, "To get out of the city, of course." Pliny would probably have given the same response, and for the same reasons that he once confided to a friend, in a letter written from Laurentum: "You should take the first opportunity yourself to leave the din, the futile bustle and useless occupations of the city." The attractions of a country retreat have changed little: peace and quiet, privacy and relaxation.

At no time was the din and bustle of the city greater than during the nineteenth century. Industrialization meant, above all, urbanization, and the growth rate for cities in Europe and America was explosive—analogous to that of Third World cities today. As national populations grew—Britain's doubled between 1800 and 1850—large numbers of rural people were obliged to move to cities and towns where expanding factories provided their only chance for gainful employment. In the early 1800s, London, with a population of about a million, was several times larger than either Vienna or Paris, and was already the largest city in the world; by the end of the century it was approaching five million. Because they were newer, American cities were smaller, but their growth was equally dramatic—the result of both a depletion of the countryside and the arrival of large numbers of European immigrants. Between 1835 and 1870, New York grew from less than two hundred thousand inhabitants to a million; Chicago's population tripled.

The rapid expansion of the nineteenth-century industrial city was bought at a great cost. Lewis Mumford likened the urban destruction and disorder of the period between 1820 and 1900 to a battlefield. Railroads cut indiscriminately through the older urban fabric, smoky factories surrounded residential areas, and inhuman slums surrounded the factories. As buildings grew higher and denser, streets became more congested. The traditional water and waste systems proved inadequate; aqueducts and underground sewers, as well as organized garbage collection, would eventually resolve these problems, but that took time.

(The first underground sewer was constructed in the 1850s, in Brooklyn; most cities did not have proper sanitation until the end of the century.) In the meantime the city became a dirty, noisy, crowded, unsafe, and unhealthy place.

Montreal was no exception. Beginning in the middle of the nineteenth century, the city underwent the first of a series of periods of spectacular growth. The change was more dramatic there than elsewhere, for when the British conquered the French colony, a hundred years earlier, Montreal had been little more than a fur-trading town with fewer than nine thousand inhabitants. With British immigration, and the influx of loyalists after the American War of Independence, the town grew to a city of twenty-two thousand by 1825. The introduction of steamships turned Montreal into the main seaport of Canada—it was soon the largest port in North America—and the Lachine Canal, built in 1825, linked ocean shipping with inland navigation from the Great Lakes. Railways joined the port to the major cities of the Eastern Seaboard, first to New York, later to Portland and Boston. Thanks to these advantages, which provided jobs for large numbers of immigrants, over the next two decades Montreal's population doubled, then doubled again. By 1910 the city contained half a million people. Twenty years later it would reach a million.

It was during this period that the newly prosperous merchant families of Montreal, like their counterparts elsewhere, began to treat themselves to second homes to escape the increasingly crowded metropolis. Some built large log houses in the Laurentian Mountains, north of the city, but these were really elaborate fishing and hunting lodges, not weekend homes. Grand family summer mansions sprang up in the suburbs, on the west end of the island of Montreal, a carriage ride of one or two hours from the city.

For some, this was not far enough. Each decade of urban growth redefined the boundaries of the city and relentlessly pushed its perimeter farther and farther into the surrounding countryside. This was typical of nineteenth-century cities, whose sheer physical extent had a major impact on urban life. It's easy to forget the small scale of the preindustrial city. Elizabethan London, for example, stretched along the Thames for little more than a mile. Going to the country was a matter of a short walk. Two hundred years later, Mozart's Vienna, with a population of roughly two hundred thousand, was still a walled city, also about a mile square; that meant that it was only a ten-minute walk to the line of fortifications, beyond which lay the country. The city of London and Vienna's Innere Stadt were densely built-up warrens of narrow streets and twisting lanes lined with tall houses built tightly one against the next. But for the inhabitants of these small, compact homes, the respite of

the open countryside was never more than a short
stroll away. This ceased to be true in the nineteenth
century, or, rather, it ceased to be universally true;
access to the now distant countryside had become a
luxury.

There were practical reasons to want to escape the
congested Victorian city. Those who had the means
had another motivation: the wish to experience the
beauties of nature, preferably in their pristine una-
dulterated state. This appreciation for the wilderness
was also something new. John Ruskin first saw the
Alps in 1833, when he was fourteen years old—and
he was overwhelmed. Describing the experience in
later life, he wrote that his emotion "belonged to the
age: a very few years—within the hundred—before
that, no child could have been born to care for mountains." Ruskin's insight is important. The Romantic
movement altered not only artistic principles but also
people's sensibilities. Mountain vistas and seashore
views, which had previously been ignored, were now
sought out as rewarding aesthetic experiences.

Montreal was an inland city, but it did have a great
river. Near Montreal, the Saint Lawrence flowed
through a flat and unattractive agricultural landscape,
but below Quebec City, as the river widened before
emptying into the Gulf, the scenery changed, and tall,
rugged cliffs produced a setting of spectacular beauty.
An additional attraction (particularly in a time when

179

air-conditioning was unknown) was the refreshing coolness of the summers. While wealthy New Yorkers were choosing the banks of the Hudson River and Newport, Rhode Island, as the site for their large summer mansions, well-to-do Montrealers fixed on the lower Saint Lawrence as their personal holiday ground. They were joined by many American visitors, who could now comfortably travel to Montreal and Quebec City by train—President Taft, for example, owned a summer house on the Saguenay River. Sir John A. Macdonald, Canada's first prime minister, also summered in the area. Resort hotels sprang up in the most picturesque spots along the north shore of the Saint Lawrence, places such as Murray Bay and Tadoussac, the site of the oldest fur-trading post in Canada. The romance of a holiday in "the wilderness," although in comfortable and well-appointed surroundings, was heightened by the nature of the transportation—the final stage of the journey was made by leisurely paddle-wheel river steamer.

The closest seacoast to Montreal was in New Brunswick, on the Bay of Fundy. Beginning in 1889, the Intercolonial Railway linked Montreal to Halifax, and it was railway tycoons, led by Sir William Van Horne, builder of the trans-Canadian line, who made Saint Andrews, a charming coastal town near the Maine border, into a favorite resort of both Bostonians and Montrealers. But even by rail, the distance to Montreal was much too great for short visits, and most people went to Saint Andrews by the Sea, as it came to be called, at the beginning of the summer and stayed for the season.

Halfway to the Maritime Provinces, about four hundred miles from Montreal, the Intercolonial Railway passed a small resort village on the south shore of the Saint Lawrence River. Metis Beach was the farthest outpost in the chain of summer resorts along the river. It had been settled by Scots, and beginning in the 1850s attracted summer visitors from Montreal. They came for the beautiful scenery, for boating and fishing, and for the fresh air—Metis Beach was advertised as having the highest level of ozone on the continent.

The first vacationers came by road, or by river steamer, but it was the railway that ensured the growth of the summer colony. Trains made travel both faster and more comfortable. The train to Montreal stopped in Metis Beach at ten o'clock in the evening and reached the city the next morning. Seeing friends and relatives off at the station on Sunday night was a weekly ritual. In its heyday, during the 1930s, Metis Beach included four hundred private homes— both cottages and mansions—nine large hotels, two golf courses and tennis clubs, four churches (all Protestant), and a library. Like Canne de Bois, the settlement stood empty during the winter, or almost so; the summer population of three thousand shrank to two hundred permanent residents.

During the early 1900s, more and more people started coming to Metis Beach by automobile. At the time this seemed like an extra convenience, but in fact the car would spell the end of the primacy of exclusive upper-class country resorts such as Metis Beach and Saint Andrews. Automobiles enabled people to travel to many more places than were served by railways or river steamers. They could, for example, if they were New Yorkers, drive to the end of Long Island, like Jay Gatsby and his friends, or into the Catskills. If they were Montrealers, they could easily visit the Laurentian Mountains or the pretty lakes in the Eastern Townships.

If the car's only role was to allow the rich to vary the location of their recreations, it would be merely a footnote in the history of the country retreat. It was not so much the car that altered leisure habits as the popularization of car ownership. The first cars were expensive and could be afforded only by the well-to-do; after 1914, when Henry Ford began mass-producing automobiles, everyone could buy a car, and did. By 1939 there was one car for every four inhabitants of the United States—the highest rate of ownership in the world (fully three quarters of all the cars in the world were owned by Americans); Canada was close behind, with a car for every eight inhabitants.* Both were far ahead of the leading European countries such as England and France (one car for every eighteen people) and the Third Reich, where there was one car for every forty-two people.

The automobile is "the most wonderful of conveniences," in historian John Lukacs's words, "not so much because of its comfort (which is limited in even the most luxurious of cars) and not even because of its reduction of distances, but because it allows its owner to be the master of his time rather than of space; he can leave whenever he wants, and return whenever he chooses; he does not depend on schedules of public transport." It is precisely this freedom that made the car the prime instrument of leisure.

Now that more and more working people had acquired a car, they also had more free time to use it. That was Henry Ford's reasoning for introducing the shorter workweek in his factories. The five-day week took longer to achieve popular acceptance than he had anticipated, but that did not diminish the attraction of car ownership. The automobile was first and foremost a plaything, not a means of transportation—that would come later. Eventually the combination of the

---

* The other leaders in automobile ownership at the time were also ex–British colonies: New Zealand (a car for every six inhabitants) and Australia (one for every nine).

two-day weekend and the automobile proved irresistible. The automobile is frequently blamed for the spread of suburbs, although the earliest planned suburban developments in America, such as Riverside, Illinois (1869), and Bronxville, New York (1890), predated the inexpensive cars and were both linked to Chicago and New York City, respectively, by railways. There is no question, however, that the automobile created a less visible extension of the city. The modern metropolis assumed a new and unexpected form: the city proper, and, many miles away, its rustic counterpart—weekend-cottage country.

Every Canadian and American city is now surrounded by a generous sprinkling of weekend settlements—a rustic mirror of itself. Or maybe a better metaphor would be the two vessels of an hourglass. Every fifth day the glass is rotated, and the sand pours from one side to the other; two days later, it is tilted again, and the sand pours back. Each Friday night, in cities across the continent, hundreds of thousands of families transpose themselves to their country retreats, to mountains, lakes, rivers, and seashores, or, as these fill up, to less picturesque sites like Canne de Bois. Unlike the nineteenth-century railway resort, cottage country is not concentrated but spread over the landscape, and it is no longer limited to the wealthy.

One shouldn't confuse cottage country with country; rural life is less affected by the weekend. Even as I write this, on a summer Saturday morning, my neighbor is hard at work, spraying his apple orchard. The weather—it looks like rain—does not allow him to wait. Nor do the cows of my other neighbor take weekend holidays; they must be attended to seven days a week. Farmers here still take their leisure according to the seasons—during the winter many go to Florida—and holidays tend to occur on rainy days—except, of course, for marriages and funerals, for which all work stops. That is to be expected, for the weekend, like the weekend retreat, is an urban habit. The two developed in tandem as consequences of city life—a time to escape, a place to escape to.

eight

Pastimes

A recent Japanese study comparing working men and women in Tokyo, New York, and Los Angeles found that although the typical time for relaxation at home after work varied from three hours (Tokyo) to four (Los Angeles) and five hours (New York), residents of all three cities named the same activity: watching television. In a similar vein, a 1989 national survey indicated that three quarters of Canadians adults reported that their major free-time activity was watching television—an average of 3.1 hours per day.

Whether it's a hot or cool medium, and whatever its lowbrow content, television has one attribute that is so obvious that it is often ignored: it is voracious. Three hours a day devoted to watching television means twenty-one hours weekly—half a workweek— a staggering and unprecedented amount of time devoted to one pastime. Few societies anywhere have ever spent so much time on a single type of amuse-

186

ment—not the Romans on their circuses (of which there were usually only eight each year), not the Middle Ages on their carnivals and feasts, not even the Georgians on their animal baiting, prizefighting, and horse racing.

There was one eighteenth-century leisure activity, however, that probably demanded almost as much time as watching television, and that was reading. Just as watching television has dramatically altered the nature of leisure in the second half of the twentieth century, so did reading books in the eighteenth. The printed book had already existed for two hundred years, but only during the 1700s did cheaper paper and faster presses—technical developments that also made possible the newspaper and the magazine—reduce printing costs enough to make books available to a larger audience.

The popularity of books was not just due to technology. Until the sixteenth century most printed books were in Latin; the international language of both clerics and scholars. Eventually translations appeared in various European languages, which meant that book reading began to spread to a broader public. Obviously, it was a public that could read. Between 1500 and 1800, literacy grew quickly in northern and northwestern Europe, which was culturally more advanced than the rest of the continent. By the mid-eighteenth century, it has been estimated that almost all the adults in some countries—Scotland, Sweden, and Denmark, for example—could read (although not necessarily write). The Reformation undoubtedly played a role, for Protestantism placed great importance on individual reading of the Scriptures; so did the growth of cities, where literacy was always higher than in the countryside, and the increasing popularity of schooling for children.

The evolution of the book as an inexpensive commodity (it had previously been a luxury) influenced its subject matter. Since printers and booksellers worked for profit, the content of books, unlike that of hand-copied manuscripts, was a direct reflection of public tastes. The first books were chiefly religious—not surprising, since most book buyers and readers were clerics; works of medieval philosophy and theology, as well as legal texts, found a smaller market among scholars and lawyers.

By the sixteenth century, people had begun to read not out of religious devotion or scholastic vocation but for pleasure. History was a popular subject, especially the classical histories of Livy, Plutarch, and Julius Caesar. According to the French historian Lucien Febvre, "The same large public which had an insatiable appetite for history, and often preferred legendary histories to objective accounts, the public which, for example, took such an interest in the legend of Troy, was equally fascinated by imaginative literature." The thirst for fiction fueled the continued popularity of medieval romances such as the *Morte d'Arthur* and the *Roman de la Rose,* and also prompted new works such as *Amadís de Gaula,* a chivalric tale of which there were more than sixty Spanish editions during the sixteenth century, and which became a best-seller throughout Europe. Eventually *Diana,* a Spanish pastoral romance by Jorge de Montemayor, and the burlesque tales of François Rabelais set the stage for the modern novel. The point has already been made that the novel signaled the arrival of a new type of leisure activity—introverted, personal, and private. What changed was not only the availability and the nature of reading material but also something else: the *way* books were read.

Between the sixteenth and eighteenth centuries more and more people acquired a new skill: the ability to read without pronouncing the words as they were read. Most people read aloud when books were rare, and many readers, lacking the ability to write, had to laboriously pick their way through the unfamiliar texts. And through unfamiliar orthography—spelling was not yet standardized and was often left to the whim of the typesetter. Moreover, reading aloud was customary; before widespread literacy, books were more often read *to* people than *by* people. Reading was a public, social activity.

Once people learned to read silently, reading became an act of quiet and solitude. Silent reading made it possible for the reader to rapidly internalize what he was reading. It was also an intensely intimate activity, as reflected in the changed subject matter of books, which now dealt with the interior life of individuals. Silent reading removed one from the surrounding world, a mental separation that eventually became physical. During the fifteenth and sixteenth centuries few people (generally churchmen or lawyers) owned private libraries. By the end of the seventeenth century, it was not unusual for a bourgeois individual such as Samuel Pepys to have a considerable collection of books, and to keep them at home in a special private room set aside for solitary reading and writing.*

The eighteenth-century study, despite its name, was less a place for study than for private relaxation. The lone figure with a book had long been a favorite subject for painters, but whereas medieval artists depicted readers who were scholars or hermits, painters like Chardin portrayed bourgeois men—and, more commonly, women—in an atmosphere of idleness and repose instead of studiousness.

The privatization of reading has been called one

---

* Silent, personal reading had a counterpart in personal writing—diaries, journals, and memoirs also made their appearance in the seventeenth century.

of the major cultural developments of the early modern era. It was also a milestone in the history of leisure. Solitary reading is the ideal vehicle for individual leisure. The reader can do something—or nothing. He can pick up one book or another. He sets the pace, reading uninterruptedly or leafing through a book at random, letting his imagination free to make what connections it will. Reading requires long periods of calm—at the comfortable rate of two hundred words a minute, it takes about fifteen hours to complete a typical novel. Reflection, contemplation, privacy, and solitude are also associated with reading books. And withdrawal. Both withdrawal from the world around one, from the cares of everyday life, and withdrawal into oneself.

The privatization of reading in the eighteenth century was nowhere as advanced as in the United States, where individual literacy was widespread and the public demand for books was correspondingly great. When Thomas Paine's anti-monarchist tract *Common Sense* was published in 1776, it sold more than a hundred thousand copies in two months. (Most editions numbered no more than two thousand copies.) In all, about four hundred thousand copies of Paine's book were eventually printed. This was in a country with a population of only 3 million persons; a book would have to sell about 24 million copies today to do as well. "Only the Super Bowl could produce such collective attention in today's America," Neil Postman ruefully observes.

There are now tens of millions of people who cannot—or do not—read books.* The large number of books published each year (more than fifty thousand titles in the United States alone) camouflages the fact that book buyers are an extremely small group, perhaps as small as ten percent of the total population. In the Canadian survey referred to at the beginning of this chapter, only eighteen percent of respondents said they read a daily newspaper, and a mere sixteen percent spent some of their leisure time reading a magazine or a book.

The criticism is often made that watching television is passive. This is true when it is compared with active recreations such as jogging or playing tennis. But watching television is no more passive than observing a landscape, listening to music, or reading a book. Like reading a book, it's a withdrawal, but a withdrawal of a different kind. Television tells a story in a way that requires no imagination; the picture on the screen and the sound provide all we need to

---

* It is estimated that as many as a third of Canadians and Americans are "functionally illiterate"; less obvious but equally disturbing is the large number of people who can read but do not—"aliterates," in Daniel Boorstin's phrase.

know—there is nothing to fill in. Television watching should more properly be called television staring; it engages eye and ear simultaneously in a relentless and persistent way and leaves no room for daydreaming. That is what makes watching television such an inferior form of leisure—not that it's passive, but that it offers so little opportunity for reflection and contemplation.

At the beach—or reading a book, or listening to Vivaldi—our attention shifts from sight to smell to sound at will. The mind wanders in and out of the scene. The physical sensations stimulate thoughts, memories, and reflections. These interruptions are an integral part of the experience of relaxing. Watching television, on the other hand, is focused, structured, and scheduled. Commercial breaks occur at preordained intervals. If the attention is distracted, the story line is lost; one cannot move in and out at will. Freedom, a key ingredient of leisure, is missing. Some latitude is restored to the viewer by the remote-control device, and even more by the videocassette recorder, which lets the viewer set the schedule and accelerate, slow, or stop the action altogether. But these are crude techniques, cruder than rereading a sentence in a book or stopping to think about what one has read. In the final analysis, compared with reading a book, television (although it is a diverting form of recreation) is a poor sort of leisure.

There's another important difference between reading a book and watching television. Serious book readers read almost daily, from habit and because of the demands of the form. A nineteenth-century novel, for example, with its dozens of characters and intertwining plots, requires close attention; it cannot be put aside for too long or the reader risks losing his place in the story. The same applies to a serious work of nonfiction, whose ordered arguments must be retained from one reading to the next. Not that books are intended to be read at one sitting; the organization of books into chapters provides convenient stopping places.

The ability to read a book presupposes the availability of short but frequently recurring periods of free time. The reduction of weekday leisure time for many people makes it difficult to find time for regular reading. Weekends don't help; they're too far apart. At least they do not help book reading, although the prevalence of intermittent, weekend reading may explain the recent explosion in the number of magazines—fast food in book-reading terms. The popularity of the blockbuster summer novels that are taken on vacation and consumed on the beach suggests that book reading has not altogether lost its attraction, only its congruity with modern leisure time.

Television's schedule is better suited to the pace of modern life. Except for daytime programs, which air daily, dramatic television programming follows a seven-day cycle. Once a week an established cast of characters enacts an independent plot, analogous to a short story. Even when a story is carried through from one week to the next—as happens with a mini-series—each show begins with flashbacks and a synopsis, as a reminder of what came before. Nor is the viewer required to follow the entire series—unlike the chapters in a book, the segments are often self-contained and can be enjoyed on their own.

The crowded work schedules of most people demand a form of leisure that can be squeezed into irregular intervals during the week—or postponed until time becomes available on the weekend. This has not had a beneficial effect on book reading, but there are leisure activities other than television watching that can also be taken up intermittently. Listening to music, for example—the entire *Four Seasons* lasts only about forty minutes. Other pastimes—stamp-collecting, building model ships, laying bricks—can also be felicitously indulged in at odd intervals, and for varying amounts of time.

Stamp collecting and model building are usually described as hobbies. "Hobby" is a curious English word that has no equivalent in other European languages. Its root, "hobbin," was medieval—like Dobbin, an affectionate name given to cart horses—and the original meaning of hobby was a small horse or

pony. A hobbyhorse also referred to the horse man-
nequins that pantomimers and morris dancers carried
around their waists. Because of this association with
play, the term was used to describe the small wooden
toy horses, some on rockers, some merely a horse's
head on a stick, that were given to young children.*
As early as the seventeenth century, "riding one's
hobbyhorse" was an expression that referred not to
children but to adults, and not to playing with a make-
believe horse but to indulging oneself in what appeared to outsiders to be a trivial pastime. Eventually,
in the nineteenth century, the noun "hobby" began
to be used to describe a particular kind of leisure
activity.

The prototypical nineteenth-century hobbyist
was a collector. The pastime of collecting things (especially old things) was a Victorian passion—the
museum was an early-nineteenth-century invention—
and well-to-do men and women amassed large col-
lections of Oriental porcelain, Japanese prints, and
other exotica. The collector of modest means collected
pressed flowers, matchboxes, and, above all, postage
stamps.

---

* Hobbyhorse was also the name given to the precursor of the
bicycle. It consisted simply of two wheels joined by a crossbar on
which the rider sat, and propelled himself forward by pushing with
his feet on the ground. Hobbyhorses were a short-lived craze in both
Europe and America at the beginning of the nineteenth century.

The first adhesive postage stamp was the famous "Penny Black," which featured a portrait of Queen Victoria and was minted in 1840. By the end of the decade, most major countries had begun to issue stamps, and people began to collect them. The earliest reference to stamp collecting occurs in 1841, in an advertisement that appeared in the London *Times*. "A young lady, being desirous of covering her dressing-room with cancelled postage stamps, has been so far encouraged in her wish by private friends as to have succeeded in collecting 16,000. These, however, being insufficient, she will be greatly obliged if any good-natured person who may have these (otherwise use-less) little articles at their disposal, would assist her in her whimsical project." Soon there were enough different varieties of stamps to use for something more interesting than wallpaper. By the early 1860s stamp collecting had become an international fad. Between 1860 and 1863, the first stamp catalogs were issued (in Belgium, Britain, France, and the United States), specialty magazines for stamp collectors appeared in several countries, a Frenchman published the first stamp album, and another Frenchman coined the term "philately," which replaced "timbromania" as the name of this popular pastime.

This kind of personalization and privatization of leisure was unusual before the nineteenth century, but it became increasingly common thereafter. "Riding one's hobbyhorse" had been a term tinged with derision, like having a bee in one's bonnet; "having a hobby" was respectable. George Santayana once characterized England as "the paradise of individuality, eccentricity, heresy, anomalies, hobbies, and humors." That was putting the hobby in the right company, for what distinguished hobbies from other recreations was that the hobbyist was devoted to his private passion out of all proportion to its real importance. It was a way of doing something and nothing at the same time.

A personal confession at this point. I had several hobbies as a boy (a model railroad, a stamp collection, a puppet theater), and I suppose that my adolescent career as a drummer qualified as a hobby, but I am always at a loss when asked to name my hobbies today. Books and music are too much a part of my everyday life to qualify as hobbies. I enjoy carpentry, but I would be just as happy to buy a bookshelf as to build one. Several years ago I tried to resuscitate my Canadian stamp collection, but I found that stamps had lost their glamour; I was merely reminded of the dismal state of the Canadian postal system. When I first acquired a personal computer, I thought that playing computer games would become a hobby; it took only a few hours of Adventure and Space Pirates to cure me of that delusion.

The closest I have come to a hobby—it is really

a weekend diversion—is rowing. This nineteenth-century pastime lets me fulfill my fascination with boats with the minimum fuss and bother. Rowing, unlike sculling, is a relaxing activity, although there is a small amount of mild physical exertion, just enough to satisfy my sedentary guilt. If you are not going far, a rowing skiff—mine is a replica of a type built in the 1920s for trout fishing on New York's Finger Lakes—is a leisurely way to go; it's less noisy than a motorboat, and considerably less complicated than a sailboat. And it allows one to share what Paul Theroux has called the secret of boating: the absolute difference of being on water instead of on land, the discovery of a different world—which is, I suppose, what hobbies are about.

What is "the purest of human pleasures . . . the greatest refreshment to the spirits of man"? The answer, according to Francis Bacon, who wrote these words in 1625, the year before his death, was not reading books or listening to music or even the diversions of a leisurely row. What the famous philosopher was describing was gardening.

Gardening is an indulgence, but it is an ancient one. The oldest work of literature in existence, the Gilgamesh Epic, mentions a landscape garden, and all the great civilizations of antiquity—the Mesopotamians, the Egyptians, the Persians, the Romans—built palace gardens of great beauty and sophistication.

These were usually grand, and resembled parks. The best-known gardens, such as those surrounding Hadrian's villa at Tivoli, were immense, and reflected the wealth of their owners. Even the landscaping of a smaller country estate like Pliny's required the labor of many workers; likewise the thirty-acre "princely" garden that Bacon proposed in his essay.

The history of the small domestic garden—as distinct from the great gardens of the aristocracy—remains to be written. It would be a task made difficult by the lack of physical evidence, for while the celebrated gardens of Isfahan, the Alhambra, and Vaux-le-Vicomte exist in nearly original form, the gardens of ordinary people of the past can be only known at second hand, from paintings or written descriptions.

There were undoubtedly modest gardens in ancient times, for at the heart of every Greek and Roman house was a courtyard surrounded by an arcade. Every room in the house would open onto this space which contained potted trees and flowers and often a pool of water. The court-garden house remained an Oriental prototype (it is also found throughout the Middle East, as well as in India) but in medieval Europe it was replaced by the narrow row house, with a garden at the rear. The ancestor of the small medieval garden was the close, or walled garden, which was initially attached to monastic buildings, a pattern derived from Byzantine churches. These cloister gardens were known as "paradises," like their Persian predecessors, and they were symbols of both the Virgin and virginity, as well as of paradise lost. Walled orchards (the Middle Ages was as security-conscious as our own time) also had romantic overtones, for they were associated with lovers' meetings.

Eventually the close became a household fixture. The walled domestic garden behind the house was almost secretive, a magical place, not least because it provided privacy. Before the home was subdivided into specialized rooms, gardens were already "refuges of intimacy," in historian Orest Ranum's charming phrase, and afforded an opportunity for the solitary contemplation of nature—especially flowers. Roses were especially popular, and, as in Pliny's time, so was the scent of violets. The flower garden (there was usually a kitchen garden elsewhere) was intended for leisure—it was specifically called a "pleasure garden"—and was the perfect place for "doing nothing." There was usually a bench, often set in an arbor, which provided a congenial setting for private conversations and romantic encounters.

Edward Hyams, the English author of *A History of Gardens and Gardening,* maintains that the seventeenth-century Dutch were the first to develop the small suburban garden. These formal gardens were miniature versions of French parterres, with clipped box hedges and extravagant topiaries; the ground was often covered in scrollwork shapes, outlined in colored earth, shells, and rocks. In the spring there were tulips, of course, but the Dutch garden, with its white-painted tree trunks, its glittering gewgaws and lifelike painted figures (also a French fashion, and the origin of the gnomes and flamingos that still decorate suburban lawns), was anything but natural. These gardens were meant for show—they were located in front of the house—not for idling, which is why, when Dutch painters wanted to portray intimate domestic scenes, they located them indoors, rarely in the garden.

All gardens are attempts to establish a happy and meaningful equilibrium between humankind and nature. According to Charles Moore, the author of *The Poetics of Gardens*, "in all of human history there seem to have emerged just two basic notions of how to do this." The first is the walled paradise garden, which keeps the outside world at bay and re-creates a perfect, orderly paradise within. The traditional walled garden of Persia was ideally a square, divided into four quarters and further subdivided by paths and watercourses. From this standard, which had endless permutations possible, came the great gardens of Islamic Spain and Mogul India. The paradise garden reoccurs in a modified but still geometric form in Renaissance Italy, and in seventeenth-century France and Holland.

The second idea, equally ancient, is of a garden ordered not according to geometry but to the natural world—asymmetrical, crooked, diversified, picturesque. Such gardens were seen first in China and Japan, and came into the European consciousness thanks to the English gardeners of the eighteenth century. They produced such masterpieces as William Kent's Rousham, begun in the 1730s. Kent, whom Horace Walpole credited with originating the new style of garden, was also an architect, but his gardening ideas were influenced by his knowledge of painting. His gardens were conceived of as a carefully orchestrated series of views—and viewing points—not only of trees and water but of many classical objects: gazebos, temples, bridges, and statues. Unlike the formal garden, whose symbolic geometry could be appreciated intellectually and at a glance, the natural English garden demanded to be walked through and seen, not just once but at different times of the day and year.

Kent and his famous successors Capability Brown and Humphry Repton were professional landscape architects, but Walpole suggested that gardening was best left to amateurs, for the owner of a garden "sees his situation in all seasons of the year, at all times of the day. He knows where beauty will not clash with convenience, and observes in his silent walks or accidental rides a thousand hints that must escape a person who in a few days sketches out a pretty picture, but has not had leisure to examine the details and relations of every part."

The eighteenth century was a period of dilettantism—Walpole himself was a noted amateur architect, whose Gothic improvements to his own house at Strawberry Hill established that style as a domestic fashion all over Europe—and nowhere was this more visible than in gardening design. John Aislabie, a politician who withdrew to Yorkshire as a result of his embroilment in the South Sea Bubble scandal, spent his latter years creating an extraordinary water garden at Studley Royal. William Shenstone, a poet and the author of *Unconnected Thoughts on Gardening,* retired to his family's country seat for his health and made a beautiful garden called "*a ferme ornēd.*" The most famous amateur gardener of the time, however, was neither a poet nor a patrician, but a banker. Henry Hoare's father had built a Palladian villa, but he died before completing the grounds. Hoare spent thirty years laying out Stourhead, a grand composition around a twenty-acre artificial lake, considered by many to be the greatest of all eighteenth-century English gardens.

Few amateur gardeners had the means to achieve works on the scale of Stourhead. Still, accessibility was one of gardening's attractions. Gardens were not just for princes or rich bankers; anyone could have a garden. This sentiment is evident in the first gardening handbook in English, the *Systema Horticulturae, or Art of Gardening*, which was published in 1677. Its author John Worlidge described the small personal gardens of his day: "There is scarce a cottage of the southern parts of England but hath its proportionable garden, so great a delight do most men take in it, that they may not only please themselves with the view of the flowers, herbs, and trees, as they grow, but furnish themselves and their neighbours upon extraordinary occasions, as nuptials, feasts, and funerals, with the proper products of their gardens." John Abercrombie's 1766 guide to gardening was explicitly aimed at the small householder—it was called *Every Man His Own Gardener*.

Small gardens, then as now, combined practicality with beauty—that is, vegetables with flowers. Chesterton once wrote that he liked his kitchen garden because it contained things to eat. There is something timelessly satisfying about digging up a potato or pulling a carrot out of the ground, and growing one's own food is undoubtedly one of the chief pleasures of gardening. The small garden remained common in the country, but town dwellers had to wait until the end of the nineteenth century and the allotment-garden movement. This movement originated in Germany and spread quickly across the Continent and to England, encouraging municipal authorities to acquire wasteland on the fringes of cities and towns and along railway tracks and make it available as small plots for the working populations who lacked their own gardens. The original aim of the movement was to provide an opportunity for healthy outdoor recreation, but allotments coincided with the advent of the Saturday half-holiday, and small suburban gardens soon became a focus for weekend leisure. They became retreats, sprouting sheds and cabins resembling dollhouses—the first weekend cottages. By the 1930s, there were more than half a million such gardens in Britain, and the number increased during World War II as a result of the "Dig for Victory" campaign.

A resurgence in allotment gardening occurred recently in Poland, where it is estimated that more than a million town households cultivate allotments and another 1.5 million are on waiting lists. The popularity of these gardens, which are often several miles outside the city, is a result of the sudden availability of free time on Saturdays and of the lack of other diversions. Growing fruits and vegetables has economic advantages, especially in Poland, where food shortages are common, but the small plots also offer people a chance to build small homemade cabins, which transform the gardens into weekend retreats. According to Anna Olszewska, a Polish sociologist, "their cultivation has become a common way of passing weekends, and they have also become sites for social and family gatherings."

In North America the growth of allotment gardening was limited by the postwar spread of single-family suburban houses, each on its own plot of land. Now everyone really could become his own gardener. In 1952, Americans spent more than a billion dollars on flowers, seeds, potted plants, and garden tools, an expenditure that had increased steadily for the previous two decades—close to twice as much as they spent on books. The 1980 census revealed that more than a hundred million Americans, more than forty percent of the population, live in suburbs. The vast majority have gardens.

The pattern elsewhere is similar. In Britain, where two thirds of all dwellings are now owner-occupied, gardening (like other home-centered hobbies) has grown steadily in popularity. A recent Hungarian survey of blue-collar workers indicates that although watching television has become the main recreation, gardening remains the chief outdoor leisure pastime. A 1978 study of the recreational use of suburban gardens in Adelaide, Australia, found that gardens were used an average of twenty-two hours a week for recreational activities in addition to gardening, and concluded that private gardens were used more intensively and flexibly than any other outdoor recreational facility in the city.

Cultivating one's own patch of ground will continue to be a popular pastime for a long time to come. Gardening fits in easily with the five-and-two timetable. Tending a garden does not require a rigid schedule, and is exactly the kind of activity that can be indulged in on weekends and at weekend country retreats. As cities become denser and more people live in apartments, it is the country place—however small—that will provide the locale for gardening. Even the small plots of land at Canne de Bois have little parcels of garden, clumps of rosebushes, or ornamental flower beds.

Gardening is undertaken voluntarily, for one's own amusement, and it fulfills Johan Huizinga's three criteria for true play: it represents freedom, it stands outside everyday life, and it contains its own course and meaning (which, like that of most play, can be serious). But it's a special kind of play. Unlike spectator sports, most games, and recreational pastimes such as dancing, gardening is not social—it is usually private. The gardener is a solitary figure, who, like the book reader, withdraws from the real world into one of his own creation.

The capacity to be alone is a valuable character trait, often associated with creative individuals. But it may have a broader application. Anthony Storr, a psychiatrist who has written about the importance of solitude in the development of creativity, maintains that any balanced person will find the meaning of his life not only in his interpersonal relationships with family and friends but also in the solitary pursuit of personal interests. Cultivating a garden may, to use Pliny's analogy, be a way to cultivate oneself.

Gardening is solitary, but it also involves outdoor physical activities (digging, planting, pruning) that make it an attractive antidote to the mechanized—and mechanical—clerical work that characterizes most modern jobs. In that sense, the garden offers possibilities for both recreation (working in the garden) *and* leisure (sitting in the garden).

Gardening is ill suited to instant gratification—a good garden cannot be rushed. Despite the cost of lawn mowers, cultivators, and seeds, gardening is not chiefly a form of consumption, and its persistence suggests that traditional leisure may be somewhat resistant to modern influences. Gardening was conveniently ignored by those critics who foretold a society increasingly obsessed with leisure goods—Veblen, for example, chose to leave gardening off his list of "conspicuous consumptions." Christopher Lasch also neglects gardening in his *Culture of Narcissism*, which argues that modern leisure is an extension of commodity production and an appendage of industry. Gardening may yet confound them both.

nine

The Problem of Leisure

In 1919 the Hungarian psychiatrist Sándor Ferenczi published a short paper entitled "Sunday Neuroses." He recounted that in his medical practice he had encountered several neurotics whose symptoms recurred on a regular basis. Although it's common for a repressed memory to return at the same time of year as the original experience, the symptoms he described appeared every week. Even more novel, they appeared most frequently on one day: Sunday. Having eliminated possible physical factors associated with Sunday, such as sleeping in, special holiday foods, and overeating, he decided that his patients' hysterical symptoms were caused by the holiday character of the day. This hypothesis seemed to be borne out by one particular case, that of a Jewish boy whose symptoms appeared on Friday evening, the commencement of the Sabbath. Ferenczi speculated that the headaches and vomiting of these holiday neurotics were a reaction to the freedom that the weekly day of rest offered. Since Sunday allowed all sorts of relaxed behavior (noisy family games, playful picnics, casual dress), Ferenczi reasoned that people who were neurotically disposed might feel uncomfortable "venting their holiday wantonness," either because they had dangerous impulses to control or because they felt guilty about letting go their inhibitions.

Ferenczi described the Sunday holiday as a day when "we are our own masters and feel ourselves free from all the fetters that the duties and compulsions of circumstances impose on us; there occurs in us—parallel with this—a kind of inner liberation also." Although "Sunday neurosis" was a clinical term, the concept of a liberation of repressed instincts coupled with a greater availability of free time raised the menacing image of a whole society running amok. Throughout the 1920s there were dozens of articles and books of a more general nature, published by psychiatrists, psychologists, and social scientists in both Europe and America, on the perils of what was often called the New Leisure. There was a widespread feeling that the working class would not really know what to do with all this extra free time.

The underlying theme was an old one: less work meant more leisure, more leisure led to idleness, and idle hands, as everyone knew, were ripe for Satan's mischief. This was precisely the argument advanced

211

by the supporters of Prohibition, who maintained that shorter hours provided workers with more free time which they would only squander on drink. Whatever the merits of this argument—and undoubtedly drinking was popular—one senses that this and other such "concerns" really masked an unwillingness to accept the personal freedom that was implicit in leisure. The pessimism of social reformers—and many intellectuals—about the abilities of ordinary people to amuse themselves has always been profound, and never more so than when popular amusements do not accord with established notions of what constitutes a good time.

In *Work Without End,* Benjamin K. Hunnicutt describes how such thinking had an important effect on reinforcing employers' opposition to the Saturday holiday in pre-Depression America. The shorter workday had eventually, and often reluctantly, been accepted by management; one reason was that studies had shown how production increased when workers had longer daily breaks and were less tired. The same did not apply, however, to the weekend. "Having Saturdays off," Hunnicutt observes, "was seen to offer the worker leisure—the opportunity to become increasingly free from the job to do other things." And if these "other things" were not good for him, then it was only proper that he should be kept in the workplace, and out of trouble.

The Depression saw this paternalistic resistance set

aside, or at least modified. Although both employers and Roosevelt's administration opposed the thirty-hour week (which effectively meant a two- or three-day weekend) proposed by labor as a work-sharing measure, the Thirty-Hour Bill was passed by Congress in 1933. The law had a two-year trial period, and was watered down by the National Industrial Recovery Act, but the pressure for some sort of work sharing was too great to ignore. Many industries adopted a shorter day and reduced the length of the workweek from six days to five.

There were different views as to what people should do with this newfound freedom. Some economists hoped the extra free time would spur consumption of leisure goods and stimulate the stagnant economy. Middle-class social reformers saw an opportunity for a program of national physical and intellectual self-improvement. That was the message of a book called *A Guide to Civilized Loafing*, written by H. A. Overstreet in 1934. Despite the title, which in later editions was changed to the more seemly *A Guide to Civilized Leisure*, the author's view was that free time was an opportunity, and the book described a daunting array of free-time activities, from amateur drama to volunteer work. Overstreet was prescient in some of his recommendations, like bicycling and hiking, although other of his enthusiasms—playing the gong, for example—have yet to catch on. If his suggestions for "loafing" seem at times obsessive, it is because there were now so many free hours to fill. Overstreet, like earlier reformers, had a narrow idea of leisure—he neglected, for example, to list two favorite American pastimes, hunting and fishing, and, despite the repeal of Prohibition, he did not mention social drinking.

The two goals of filling leisure time—one economic and one cultural—appeared to many to be incompatible. Walter Lippmann's 1930 article in *Woman's Home Companion* entitled "Free Time and Extra Money" articulated "the problem of leisure." He warned that leisure offered the individual difficult choices, choices for which a work-oriented society such as America had not prepared him.* Lippmann was concerned that if people didn't make creative use of their free time, it would be squandered on mass entertainments and commercial amusements. His view spawned many books and articles of popular sociology with titles such as *The Challenge of Leisure*, *The Threat of Leisure*, and even *The Menace of Leisure*.

Much of this concern was based on the widespread assumption that the amount of available free time was greater than ever, and that the "problem of leisure"

---

* More than a quarter century later, in *The Human Condition*, Hannah Arendt echoed this view: "What we are confronted with is the prospect of a society of laborers without labor, that is, without the only activity left to them. Surely, nothing could be worse."

was without precedent. Before the Depression, an American working a forty-hour week spent less than half his 5,840 waking hours each year on the job— the rest was free time. By comparison, a hundred years earlier, work had accounted for as much as two thirds of one's waking hours. But as Hannah Arendt observed, this reduction is misleading, since the modern period was inevitably measured against the Industrial Revolution, which represented an all-time low as far as the number of working hours was concerned. A comparison with earlier periods of history leads to a different conclusion. The fourth-century Roman, for example, with 175 annual public holidays, spent fewer than a third of his waking hours at work; in medieval Europe, religious festivals reduced the work year to well below the modern level of two thousand hours. Indeed, until the eighteenth century, Europeans and Americans enjoyed *more* free time than they do today. The American worker of the 1930s was just catching up.

Most critics however, preferred to look to the future. What they saw was further mechanization, as well as technological innovations such as automation, which promised continued gains in efficiency and productivity in the workplace. "The old world of oppressive toil is passing, and we enter now upon new freedom for ourselves . . . in an age of plenty, we can look forward to an increasing amount of time that is our own." Overstreet wrote this the year after the Thirty-Hour Bill was passed, and to him, as to many others, it appeared that the shortening of the working day was a trend that would continue for some time. "It would be a rash prophet who denies the possibility that this generation may live to see a two-hour day," wrote another observer.

How wrong they turned out to be. Working hours bottomed out during the Depression, and then started to rise again. Job creation, not work sharing, became the goal of the New Deal. By 1938 the Thirty-Hour Bill had expired and the Fair Labor Standards Act provided for a workweek of not thirty but forty hours. As Hunnicutt observes, this marked the end of a century-long trend. On the strength of the evidence of the last fifty years, it would appear that the trend has not only stopped but reversed. In 1948, thirteen percent of Americans with full-time jobs worked more than forty-nine hours a week; by 1979 the figure had crept up to eighteen percent. Ten years later, the Bureau of Labor Statistics estimated that of 88 million Americans with full-time jobs, fully twenty-four percent worked more than forty-nine hours a week.

Ask anyone how long they spend at work and they can tell you exactly; it is more difficult to keep track of leisure. For one thing, it is irregular; for another, it varies from person to person. For some, cutting the lawn is a burden; for others it is a pleasurable pastime. Going to the mall can be a casual Saturday outing, or it can be a chore. Most would count watching television as leisure, but what about Sunday brunch? Sometimes the same activity—walking the dog—can be a pleasure, sometimes not, depending on the weather. Finally, whether an activity is part of our leisure depends as much on our frame of mind as anything else.

Surveys of leisure habits often show diverging results. Two recent surveys, by the University of Maryland and by Michigan's Survey Research Center, both suggest that most Americans enjoy about thirty-nine hours of leisure time weekly. On the other hand, a 1988 survey conducted by the National Research Center of the Arts came to a very different conclusion and found that "Americans report a median 16.6 hours of leisure time each week." The truth is probably somewhere in between.

Less surprising, given the number of people working more than forty-nine hours a week, was the National Research Center's conclusion that most Americans have suffered a decline in weekly leisure time of 9.6 hours over the last fifteen years. The nineteenth-century activists who struggled so hard for a shorter workweek and more free time would have been taken aback by this statistic—what had happened to the "Eight Hours for What We Will"?

There are undoubtedly people who work longer hours out of personal ambition, to escape problems at home, or from compulsion. The term "workaholic" (a postwar Americanism) is recent, but addiction to work is not—Thomas Jefferson, for example, was a compulsive worker, as was G. K. Chesterton—and there is no evidence that there are more such people today than in the past. Of course, for many, longer hours are not voluntary—they are obliged to work more merely to make ends meet. This has been particularly true since the 1970s, when poverty in America began to increase, but since the shrinking of leisure time began during the prosperous 1960s, economic need isn't the only explanation.

Twenty years ago Staffan Linder, a Swedish sociologist, wrote a book about the paradox of increasing affluence and decreasing leisure time in the United States. Following in Lippmann's steps, Linder observed that in a prosperous consumer society there was a conflict between the market's promotion of luxury goods and the individual's leisure time. When work hours were first shortened, there were few luxury items available to the general public, and the extra free time was generally devoted to leisure. With the growth of the so-called "leisure industry," people were offered a choice: more free time or more spending? Only the wealthy could have both. If the average person wanted to indulge in expensive recreations such as skiing or sailing, or to buy expensive entertainment devices, it would be necessary to work more—to trade his or her free time for overtime or a second job. Whether because of the effectiveness of advertising or from simple acquisitiveness, most people chose spending over more free time.

Linder's thesis was that economic growth caused an increasing scarcity of time, and that statistics showing an increase in personal incomes were not necessarily a sign of growing prosperity. People were earning more because they were working more. A large percentage of free time was being converted into what he called "consumption time," and mirrored a shift from "time-intensive" to "goods-intensive" leisure. According to *U.S. News & World Report,* Americans now spend more than $13 billion annually on sports clothing; put another way, about 1.3 billion hours of potential leisure time are exchanged for leisure wear—for increasingly elaborate running shoes, certified hiking shorts, and monogrammed warm-up suits. In 1989, to pay for these indulgences, more workers than ever before—6.2 percent—held a second, part-time job; in factories, overtime work increased to an average of four hours a week, the highest number in nearly twenty years.

Probably the most dramatic change is the large-scale entry of women into the labor force. In 1950 only thirty percent of American women worked outside the home, and this primarily out of economic necessity. Beginning in the 1960s middle-class women, dissatisfied with their suburban isolation and willing to trade at least some of their leisure time for purchasing power, started to look for paid employment. By 1986 more than half of all adult women— including married women with children—worked outside the home. Nor are these trends slowing down; between 1980 and 1988, the number of families with two or more wage earners rose from 19 to 21 million.

"Working outside the home" is the correct way to describe the situation, for housework (three or four hours a day) still needs to be done. Whether it is shared, or, more commonly, falls on the shoulders of women as part of their "second shift," leisure time for one or both partners is drastically reduced. Moreover, homes are larger than at any time in the postwar period, and bigger houses also mean more time spent in cleaning, upkeep, and repairs.*

Even if one chooses to consume less and stay at home, there are other things that cut into free time. Commuting to and from work takes longer than it

---

* The average size of a new American home in the 1950s was less than 1,000 square feet; by 1983 it had increased to 1,710 square feet, and in 1986 had expanded another 115 square feet.

used to. So does shopping—the weekly trip to the mall consumes more time than a stroll to the neighborhood corner store. Decentralized suburban life, which is to say American life, is based on the automobile. Parents become chauffeurs, ferrying their children back and forth to dance classes, hockey games, and the community pool. At home, telephone answering machines have to be played back, the household budget entered into the personal computer, the lawn mower dropped off at the repair shop, the car—or cars—serviced. All these convenient labor-saving devices relentlessly eat into our discretionary time. For many executives, administrators, and managers, the reduction of leisure time is also the result of office technology that brings work to the home. Fax machines, paging devices, and portable computers mean that taking work home at night is no longer difficult or voluntary. Even the contemplative quiet of the morning automobile commute is now disrupted by the presence of the cellular telephone.

There is no contradiction between the surveys that indicate a reversing trend, resulting in less free time, and the claim that the weekend dominates our leisure. Longer work hours and more overtime cut mainly into weekday leisure. So do longer commuting, driving the kids, and Friday-night shopping. The weekend—or what's left of it, after Saturday household chores—is when we have time to relax.

But the weekend has imposed a rigid schedule on our free time, which can result in a sense of urgency ("soon it will be Monday") that is at odds with relaxation. The weekly rush to the cottage is hardly leisurely, nor is the compression of various recreational activities into the two-day break. The freedom to do something has become the obligation to do something, just as Chesterton foretold, and the list of dutiful recreations includes strenuous disciplines intended for self-improvement (fitness exercises, jogging, bicycling), competitive sports (tennis, golf), and skill-testing pastimes (sailing, skiing).

Recreations such as tennis or sailing are hardly new, but before the arrival of the weekend, for most people, they were chiefly seasonal activities. Once a year, when vacation time came around, tennis racquets were removed from the back of the cupboard, swimwear was taken out of mothballs, skis were dusted off. The accent was less on technique than on having a good time. It was like playing Scrabble at the summer cottage: no one remembers all the rules, but everyone can still enjoy the game. Now the availability of free time every weekend has changed this casual attitude. The very frequency of weekend recreations allows continual participation and continual improvement, which encourage the development of proficiency and skill.

Skill is necessary since difficulty characterizes modern recreations. Many nineteenth-century amusements, such as rowing, were not particularly involved and required little instruction; mastering windsurfing, on the other hand, takes considerable practice and dexterity—which is part of the attraction. Even relatively simple games are complicated by the need to excel. Hence the emphasis on professionalism, which is expressed by the need to have the proper equipment and the correct costume (especially the right shoes). The desire for mastery isn't limited to outdoor recreations; it also includes complicated hobbies such as woodworking, electronics, and automobile restoration. All this suggests that the modern weekend is characterized by not only the sense of obligation to do something but the obligation to do it *well*.

The desire to do something well, whether it is sailing a boat—or building a boat—reflects a need that was previously met in the workplace. Competence was shown on the job—holidays were for messing around. Nowadays the situation is reversed. Technology has removed craft from most occupations. This is true in assembly-line jobs, where almost no training or experience, hence no skill, is required, as well as in most service positions (store clerks, fast-food attendants) where the only talent required is to learn how to smile and say "have a good day." But it's also increasingly true in such skill-dependent work as house construction, where the majority of parts come ready-made from the factory and the carpenter merely assembles them, or automobile repair, which consists largely in replacing one throwaway part with another. Nor is the reduction of skills limited to manual work. Memory, once the prerequisite skill of the white-collar worker, has been rendered superfluous by computers; teachers, who once needed dramatic skills, now depend on mechanical aids such as slide projectors and video machines; in politics, oratory has been killed by the thirty-second sound bite.

Hence an unexpected development in the history of leisure. For many, weekend free time has become not a chance to escape work but a chance to create work that is more meaningful—to work at recreation—in order to realize the personal satisfactions that the workplace no longer offers.

"Leisure" is the most misunderstood word in our vocabulary. We often use the words "recreation" and "leisure" interchangeably—recreation room, rest and recreation, leisure suit, leisure industry—but they really embody two different ideas. Recreation carries with it a sense of necessity and purpose. However pleasurable this antidote to work may be, it's a form of active employment, engaged in with a specific end in mind—a refreshment of the spirit, or the body, or both. Implicit in this idea of renewal—usually organized renewal—is the notion that recreation is both a consequence of work and a preparation for more of it.

Leisure is different. That was what Lippmann was getting at when he contrasted commercial recreation with individual leisure. Leisure is not tied to work the way that recreation is—leisure is self-contained. The root of the word is the Latin *licere* which means "to be permitted," suggesting that leisure is about freedom. But freedom for what? According to Chesterton's cheerful view, leisure was above all an opportunity to do nothing. When he said "doing nothing," however, he was describing not emptiness but an occasion for reflection and contemplation, a chance to look inward rather than outward. A chance to tend one's garden, as Voltaire put it. That is why Chesterton called this kind of leisure "the most precious, the most consoling, the most pure and holy."

Bertrand Russell placed leisure into a larger historical context in his essay "In Praise of Idleness." "Leisure is essential to civilization," he wrote, "and in former times leisure for the few was only rendered possible by the labours of the many. But their labours were valuable, not because work is good, but because leisure is good." Russell, a member of the aristocracy, pointed out that it had been precisely the leisure classes, not the laborers, who had written the books, invented the philosophies, produced the sciences, and cultivated the arts. But he was not arguing for a continuation of the class system; on the contrary, he proposed extending the leisure that had previously been reserved for the few to the many. This was an explicit attack on the work ethic, which he considered a device to trick people into accepting a life without leisure. In his view, the trick hadn't succeeded; working men and women had no illusions about work—they understood it was merely a necessary means to a livelihood.

Russell's underlying argument was that we should free ourselves from the guilt about leisure that modern society has imposed on us. Hence the use of terms such as "idleness" and "doing nothing," which were intended as a provocation to a society that placed the highest value on "keeping busy." Both Russell and Chesterton agreed with Aristotle, who considered leisure the aim of life. "We work," he wrote, "to have leisure."

"In Praise of Idleness" was written in 1932, at the height of the Depression, and Russell's proposal of a four-hour workday now appears hopelessly utopian. But the weekend's later and sudden new popularity in so many societies suggests that leisure is beginning to make a comeback, although not as fully as Russell desired, nor in so relaxed a way as Chesterton would have wished. I cannot shake the suspicion that something more than mere functionality accounts for the widespread popularity of the weekend. Can its universal appeal be explained by a resonance with some ancient inclination, buried deep in the human psyche? Given the mythological roots of the planetary week, and the devotional nature of Sunday and the Sabbath, the answer is likely to be found in early religious attitudes.

Mircea Eliade, a historian of religion, characterized traditional premodern societies as experiencing the world in two distinct ways corresponding to two discontinuous modes of being: the sacred and the profane. According to Eliade, the sacred manifested itself in various ways—how physical space was perceived, for example. The profane, chaotic world, full of menace, was given structure and purpose by the existence of fixed, meaningful sacred places. Sacred places could occur in the landscape, beside holy trees or on certain mountains, but they could also be man-made. Hence the elaborate rituals practiced by all ancient people when they founded settlements and erected buildings, rituals not only to protect the future town or building but to delineate a sacred space.

The prime sacred space was the home, for houses were not merely shelters but consecrated places that incorporated cosmic symbolism into their very construction. The Navajo Indians, for example, affirmed that their homes—hogans—were based on a divine prototype. The conical shape of the hogan resembled

227

a mountain in New Mexico that the Navajo called "the heart of the Earth." They believed that God had created the first forked-stick hogan using posts made of white shell, turquoise, abalone, and obsidian. When a new hogan was built, pieces of these four minerals were buried beneath the four main posts, which also corresponded to the four points of the compass. In this way the builder interrupted the continuity of the everyday world by creating a separate magical space.

A person stepping out of the desert sun into the dark, cool interior of a hogan was entering a space that was a part of the ancient past, and thus he was entering not only a sacred space but a sacred time. According to Eliade, profane time was ordinary temporal duration, but sacred time, which was also the time of festivals and holy days, was primordial and mythical, and stood apart from everyday life. During sacred time, the clock not only stopped, it was turned back. The purpose of religious rites was precisely to reintegrate this past into the present. In this way, sacred time became part of a separate, repetitive continuum, "an eternal mythical present."

Eliade characterized modern Western society as "nonreligious," in the sense that it had desacralized and demythologized the world. For nonreligious man there could be only profane space and profane time. But, he pointed out, since the roots of this society lay in a religious past, it could never divest itself completely of ancient beliefs; remnants of these remained, although in camouflaged form: for example, movies employing mythical motifs, such as the struggle between hero and monster, descent into an underworld, or the cleansing ordeal. Even in our homes, which no longer incorporate cosmic symbolism in the comprehensive way of the Navajo hogan, rituals have not altogether disappeared. Giving a housewarming party, carrying the bride over the threshold, receiving important guests at the front door instead of at the back door, decorating the exterior at festal times of year—these are all reminders that although we treat our houses as commodities, the home is still a special space, standing apart from the practical world.

Is it fanciful to propose that the repetitive cycle of week and weekend is a modern paraphrase of the ancient opposition of profane and sacred time? Obviously the weekend is not a historical remnant in any literal sense, since it didn't even exist until the nineteenth century, and its emergence was in response to specific social and economic conditions. Nor am I suggesting that the secular weekend is a substitute for religious festivals, although it is obviously linked to religious observance. But there are several striking parallels.

Weekday time, like profane time, is linear. It represents an irreversible progression of days, Monday to Friday, year after year. Past weekday time is lost time. Schooldays are followed by workdays, the first job by the second and the third. I can never be a

229

schoolboy again, or a college student, or a young architect anxiously waiting to meet my first client.* Not only is weekday time linear, but, like profane time, it encompasses the unpredictable. During the week, unforeseen things happen. People get promoted and fired. Stock markets soar or crash. Politicians are elected or voted out of office. One has the impression that history occurs on weekdays.†

The weekend, on the other hand, is, in Plato's words, a time to take a breather. It's a time apart from the world of mundane problems and mundane concerns, from the world of making a living. On weekends time stands still, and not only because we take off our watches. Just as holidays at the beach are an opportunity to re-create our childhood, to build sand castles with the kids, to paddle in the surf, to lie on the sand and get a sunburn, many of the things we do on weekends correspond to the things we did on weekends past. Weekend time shares this sense of reenactment with sacred time, and just as sacred time was characterized by ritual, the weekend, despite

---

* Several years ago I attended a high-school class reunion, which could be described as an attempt to recover weekday time. Revealingly, the subject of conversation was sports and extracurricular activities, not what we had done in the classroom.

† The notable exception is war, which often begins on the weekend, when it is least expected. The German blitzkrieg of 1940 was launched on a Saturday morning; the Japanese attack on Pearl Harbor occurred on a Sunday; the Egyptians started the Yom Kippur War on the Sabbath.

being an opportunity for personal freedom, is governed by convention: raking leaves, grilling steaks on the barbecue, going to the movies, Saturday night out, reading the Sunday paper, brunch, the afternoon opera broadcast, weekend drives, garage sales, weekend visits. The predictability of the weekend is one of its comforts.

Although Eliade described examples of sacred time from different societies and periods of history, the specific rites and rituals varied. An event could be holy in one culture and have no meaning in another; a festival could be a taboo time because the day was considered unlucky, while elsewhere it was observed for exactly the opposite reason. The myths of their sacred histories differentiated societies.

The conventions of weekend leisure, too, vary from place to place. In Europe, for example, northerners read more books than southerners, Germans and Danes spend more than others on musical instruments, the British are the greatest gamblers, the Italians the greatest moviegoers, and everyone favors tennis except the French. Canada and the United States, which have many similarities, differ in their attitude to leisure, and surveys have consistently shown that Americans believe more strongly in the work ethic than Canadians do. Probably for that reason, Canadians give personal leisure a higher importance and have been much slower to accept commercial intrusions such as Sunday shopping.

The differences in national attitudes toward leisure are arresting because we live in a world where the character of work is increasingly international. Around the world, in different countries, what happens between nine and five during the week is becoming standardized. Because of international competition and transnational ownership of companies, the transfer of technology from one country to another is almost instantaneous. All offices contain the same telephones, photocopiers, word processors, computers, and fax machines. The Japanese build automobile plants in the United States and Canada, the Americans build factories in Eastern Europe, the Europeans in South America. Industries are increasingly dominated by a diminishing number of extremely large and similar corporations. The reorganization of the workplace in Communist and formerly Communist countries, along more capitalist lines, is one more step in the standardization of work. And as work becomes more standardized, and international, one can expect that leisure, by contrast, will be even more national, more regional, more different.

Leisure has always been partly a refuge from labor. The weekend, too, is a retreat from work, but in a different way: a retreat from the abstract and the universal to the local and the particular. In that sense, leisure is likely to continue to be, as Pieper claimed, the basis of culture. Every culture chooses a different structure for its work and leisure, and in doing so it makes a profound statement about itself. It invents, adapts, and recombines old models, hence the long list of leisure days: public festivals, family celebrations, market days, taboo days, evil days, holy days, feasts, Saint Mondays and Saint Tuesdays, commemorative holidays, summer vacations—and weekends.

The weekend is our own contribution, another way of dealing with the ancient duality. The institution of the weekend reflects the many unresolved contradictions in modern attitudes toward leisure. We want to have our cake, and eat it too. We want the freedom to be leisurely, but we want it regularly, every week, like clockwork. The attraction of Saint Monday was that one could "go fishing" when one willed; the regularity of the weekend—every five days—is at odds with the ideas of personal freedom and spontaneity. There is something mechanical about this oscillation, which creates a sense of obligation that interferes with leisure. Like sacred time, the weekend is comfortingly repetitive, but the conventionality of weekend free time, which must exist side by side with private pastimes and idiosyncratic hobbies, often appears restrictive. "What did you do on the weekend?" "The usual," we answer, mixing dismay with relief.

We have invented the weekend, but the dark cloud of old taboos still hangs over the holiday, and the combination of the secular with the holy leaves us uneasy. This tension only compounds the guilt that many of us continue to feel about not working, and leads to the nagging feeling that our free time should be used for some purpose higher than having fun. We want leisure, but we are afraid of it too.

Do we work to have leisure, or the other way around? Unsure of the answer, we have decided to keep the two separate. If C. P. Snow had not already used the term in another context, it would be tempting to speak of Two Cultures. We pass weekly from one to the other—from the mundane, communal, increasingly impersonal, increasingly demanding, increasingly bureaucratic world of work to the reflective, private, controllable, consoling world of leisure. The weekend; our own, and not our own, it is what we wait for all week long.

Acknowledgments

I have wanted to write a book on leisure for several years—my earliest outline dates from 1986. Another book intruded itself in the meantime, but I must admit that I was happy to be distracted for I was having trouble getting started. Since Veblen broached the subject, in 1899, so much has been written on leisure that the subject appeared to me exhausted, wrung out, mined dry. Still, the matter nagged. I am not sure why leisure held such a fascination—perhaps because I tended to agree with Noël Coward, who said, "Work is more fun than fun." I enjoyed my work, but one couldn't work all the time, and what exactly was the meaning of the periods in between? Were they really just rest periods, or something more? It was as a result of the encouragement, prodding, and raised eyebrows of Carl Brandt, who is also my agent, that I persevered. I exchanged several letters with John Lukacs on the subject, and his observations were stimulating, as always. Dan Frank, at Viking, was both

235

gently critical and supportive, in turn. For a splendid job of copyediting, my thanks to Harriet Brown. Lastly, my appreciation to the helpful staff of McGill University's McLennan Graduate Library.

March 1989–December 1990

Notes on Sources

This is not intended to be a work of research, more like an extended essay. Nevertheless, I have relied on the work of many scholars, and it seems only fair to gratefully acknowledge my chief sources.

1: Free Time

Information on Vivaldi is from Marc Pincherle's *Vivaldi: Genius of the Baroque* (trans. Christopher Hatch, New York, 1962). Background on the history of the Sunday paper is from Sidney Kobre's *Development of American Journalism* (Dubuque, Iowa, 1969). G. K. Chesterton's essay, "On Leisure," is contained in *Generally Speaking* (London, 1928). Churchill's brick-laying is described by William Manchester in *The Last Lion: Winston Spencer Churchill, Visions of Glory, 1874–1932* (Boston, 1983). Lewis Mumford's views of meaningful work are contained in *The Pentagon of Power* (New York, 1964). Anyone interested in the relationship between leisure and work is obliged to read Josef Pieper, chiefly *Leisure: The Basis of Culture* (trans. Alexander Dru, New York, 1952), and *In Tune with the World: A Theory of Festivity* (trans. Richard and Clara Winston, Chicago, 1965).

2: Week After Week

Information on the origin of the seven-day week is drawn largely from F. H. Colson's delightful *The Week: An Essay on the Origin and Development of the Seven-Day Cycle* (Cambridge, 1926), and from Hutton Webster's classic *Rest Days* (New York, 1916); also from *Hidden Rhythms: Schedules and Calendars in Social Life* (Chicago 1981) and *The Seven Day Cycle* (New York, 1985), both by Eviatar Zerubavel. On ancient calendars I have consulted Benjamin D. Meritt's *The Athenian Year* (Berkeley & Los Angeles, 1961), Agnes Kirsopp Michels's *The Calendar of the Roman Republic* (Princeton, 1967), W. M. O'Neil's *Time and the Calendars* (Sydney, 1978), David S. Landes's *Revolution in Time: Clocks and the Making of the Modern World* (Cambridge, Mass., 1983), and Daniel J. Boorstin's *The Discoverers* (New York, 1983).

The French revolutionary calendar is described by Simon Schama in *Citizens: A Chronicle of the French Revolution* (New York, 1989); details on Soviet efforts to restructure the week are from *Soviet Labour and Industry* (London, 1942) by Leonard E. Hubbard. Jeremy Campbell outlines recent discoveries in chronobiology in *Winston Churchill's Afternoon Nap: A Wide-Awake Inquiry into the Human Nature of Time* (New York, 1986).

3: A Meaningful Day

Hannah Arendt's observations on work are contained in *The Human Condition* (Chicago, 1958). The number of holidays in various cultures is drawn chiefly from Hutton Webster; the results of the study of Tokyo residents' vacation time was reported by the *Montreal Gazette:* "Tokyoites more tired, stressed than residents of N.Y. or L.A." (July 31, 1989). The World War I study on longer hours is contained in S. Howard Bartley and Eloise Chute's *Fatigue and Impairment in Man* (New York, 1947); on the subject of fatigue: Angelo Mosso's *Fatigue* (trans. Margaret Drummond and W. B. Drummond, New York, 1906), and the more recent *Psychological Aspects and Physiological Correlates of Work and Fatigue* (Ernst Simonson and Philip

C. Weiser, eds., Springfield, Ill., 1976); the British author who observed the production fall-off at the end of the week is Donald Scott in *The Psychology of Work* (London, 1970). On tabooed days, I have (again) relied on Hutton Webster; Thorstein Veblen's book is, of course, *The Theory of the Leisure Class* (New York, 1979). The various traditions of the market week are chiefly from Martin P. Nilsson's *Primitive Time-Reckoning* (Lund, 1920), also F. E. Forbes's *Dahomey and the Dahomans* (London, 1851), and C. R. Markham's *First Part of the Royal Commentaries of the Yncas* (London, 1871). Colonial American Sabbatarianism is described by Winton U. Solberg in *Redeem the Time: The Puritan Sabbath in Early America* (Cambridge, Mass., 1977). The debate over Sunday-observance in Quebec is recounted by David Rome in two monographs: *On Sunday Observance, 1906* (Canadian Jewish Archives No. 14, Montreal, 1979) and *The Jewish Archival Record of 1936* (Canadian Jewish Archives, No. 8, Montreal, 1978). It is also referred to by W. D. K. Kernaghan in his unpublished Ph.D. thesis, *Freedom of Religion in the Province of Quebec, with Particular Reference to the Jews, Jehovah's Witnesses and Church-State Relations 1930–1960* (Duke University, 1966).

4: Sunday in the Park

There are many sources for material on Seurat; I have consulted John Russell's *Seurat* (London, 1965), and *Seurat* (Oxford, 1985) by Richard Thomson, whose analysis of *Grand Jatte* I have drawn on. For information on Parisian life of the time I have consulted Eugen Weber's admirable *France, Fin de Siècle* (Cambridge, Mass., 1986). Scholarly research on leisure in eighteenth-century England is prolific. I refer to Hugh Cunningham's *Leisure in the Industrial Revolution* (New York, 1980), and much of the material is drawn from two outstanding essays by J. H. Plumb: "The Public, Literature, and the Arts in the Eighteenth Century" (in *The Emergence of Leisure*, Michael R. Marrus, ed., New York, 1974) and "The Commercialization of Leisure in Eighteenth-century England" (in Neil McKendrick et al., *The Birth of a Consumer Society*, Bloomington, Indiana, 1982). The history of the circus is described by Ruth Manning-Sanders in *The English Circus* (London, 1952). On food and drink: J. C. Drummond and Anne Wilbraham's *The Englishman's Food: A History of Five Centuries of English Diet* (London, 1939), and Fernand Braudel's *The Structures of Everyday Life: The Limits of the Possible* (trans. Sian Reynolds, New York, 1981).

5: Keeping Saint Monday

Much of the historical material in this chapter is drawn from Douglas A. Reid's essay, "The Decline of Saint Monday 1766–1876" (*Past and Present*, 71, 1976). Other sources for the Saint Monday tradition and eighteenth-century leisure are: E. P. Thompson's "Time, Work-Discipline, and Industrial Capitalism" (*Past & Present*, 38, 1967), and Michael R. Marrus's "Introduction" to *The Emergence of Leisure* (Michael R. Marrus, ed., New York, 1974). Thomas Wright's contemporary account is *Some Habits and Customs of the Working Classes by a Journeyman Engineer* (London, 1867). On the Early Closing Association, Wilfred B. Whitaker's *Victorian and Edwardian Shopworkers: The Struggle to Obtain Better Conditions and a Half-Holiday* (Newton Abbot, 1973); and on Victorian leisure, Peter Bailey's *Leisure and Class in Victorian England* (London, 1978), Ralph Dutton's *The Victorian Home* (London, 1954), and Colin MacInnes's charming *Sweet Saturday Night* (London, 1967), which is the source for the music-hall song.

6: A World of Weekends

On the shortening of the American work week, I have relied on Joseph S. Zeisel's "The Workweek in American Industry 1850–1956" (*Monthly Labor Review*, 81, January, 1958), Daniel T. Rodgers's *The Work Ethic in Industrial America 1850–1920* (Chicago, 1974), David R. Roediger and Philip S. Foner's *Our Own Time: A History of American Labor and the Working Day* (New York, 1989), Roy Rosenzweig's *Eight Hours for What We Will: Workers and Leisure in an Industrial City, 1870–1920* (Cambridge, 1983), and Marion Cotter Cahill's *Shorter Hours: A Study of the Movement Since the Civil War* (New York, 1932). The social study of Westchester County is contained in *Leisure: A Suburban Study* (New York, 1934) by George A. Lundberg, Mirra Komarovsky, and Mary Alice McInery. On the early history of the movies: Lary May's *Screening Out the Past: The Birth of Mass Culture and the Motion Picture Industry* (New York, 1980). Benjamin Kline Hunnicutt's valuable study, *Work Without End: Abandoning Shorter Hours for the Right to Work* (Philadelphia, 1988), provides an overview of the period 1920–1940. For the emergence of the fascist Saturday, I am indebted to Victoria de Grazia's fascinating study, *The Culture of Consent: Mass Organization of Leisure in Fascist Italy* (Cambridge, 1981); the German material was based on L. Hamburger's *How Nazi Germany Has Mobilized and Controlled Labor* (Washington, D.C., 1940), Richard Grunberger's *The 12-Year Reich: A Social History of Nazi Germany 1933–1945* (New York, 1971), and Wallace R. Deuel's *People under Hitler* (New York, 1942). For European information on leisure I relied on Anthony Edwards's *Leisure Spending in the European Community: Forecasts to 1990* (London, January 1981); on the French weekend, Joffre Dumazedier's *Sociology of Leisure* (trans. Marea A. McKenzie, Amsterdam, 1974); on Israel, Elihu Katz and Michael Gurevitch's *The Secularization of Leisure: Culture and Communication in Israel* (London, 1976). For the appearance of the Polish weekend, on Neal Ascherson's *The Polish August: The Self-Limiting Revolution* (New York, 1981) and Anna Olszewska's "Poland: The Impact of the Crisis on Leisure Patterns" in *Leisure and Lifestyle: A Comparative Analysis of Free Time* (Anna Olszewska and K. Roberts, eds., London, 1989). The last anthology also contains a useful essay on Japanese leisure: Sampei Koseki's "Japan: Homo Ludens Japonicus." In addition, not being able to visit Japan, I gleaned useful information from Herman Kahn and Thomas Pepper's *The Japanese Challenge: The Success and Failure of Economic Success* (New York, 1980), Ezra F. Vogel's sociological study, *Japan's New Middle Class: The Salary Man and His Family in a Tokyo Suburb* (Berkeley, Calif., 1963), Jared Taylor's *Shadows of the Rising Sun: A Critical View of the "Japanese Miracle"* (New York, 1983), James Allen Dator's "The 'Protestant Ethic' in Japan" in *Selected Readings on Modern Japanese Society* (George K. Yamamoto and Tsuyoshi Ishida, eds., Berkeley, Calif., 1971), "Protection Racket," *The New Republic* (202, 18, April 30,

1990), and James Fallows's insightful "The Hard Life," *Atlantic* (263, 3, March, 1989).

7: Retreats

John Habraken drew the parallel between shanty-towns and campgrounds in "Aap Noot Mies Huis/ Three R's for Housing," *Forum* (XX, December 1, 1966). The description of Pliny's seaside villa is contained in Book II, Letter XVII of *The Letters of Pliny the Younger* (trans. Betty Radice, Harmondsworth, 1969); Leon Battista Alberti's views on country houses are contained in *On the Art of Building in Ten Books* (trans. Joseph Rykwert et al., Cambridge, Mass., 1988). The Mumford reference appears in *The City in History: Its Origins, Its Transformations, and Its Prospects* (New York, 1961). On the summer houses of Victorian Montrealers, see France Gagnon Pratte's *Country Houses for Montrealers 1892–1924: The Architecture of E. and W. S. Maxwell* (trans. Linda Blythe, Montreal, 1987). The material on Metis Beach is drawn from Jessie Forbes's unpublished *Metis Beach Past and Present* (undated) and from Samuel Mathewson Baylis's *Enchanting Metis* (Montreal, 1928). Metis Beach survives today, but in much diminished form. The grand hotels are all gone; only a few of the original families maintain their country homes. I have quoted John Lukacs from his absorbing and stimulating *Outgrowing Democracy: A History of the United States in the Twentieth Century* (Garden City, N.Y., 1984).

8: Pastimes

The comparative study of Japanese and American cities was reported in "Tokyoites more tired, stressed than residents of N.Y. or L.A." (*Montreal Gazette,* July 31, 1989); Canadian data is from "How long does it take a Canadian to get through the day?" (*Montreal Gazette,* March 20, 1989). I consulted Lucien Febvre and Henri-Jean Martin's *The Coming of the Book: The Impact of Printing 1450–1800* (trans. David Gerard, London, 1976), and Yves Castin's fascinating "Figures of Modernity" in *A History of Private Life: Passions of the Renaissance* (Roger Chartier, ed., trans. Arthur Goldhammer, Cambridge, Mass., 1989), on the early history of the book. Neil Postman's vigorous critique of modern American culture is *Amusing Ourselves to Death: Public Discourse in the Age of Show Business* (New York, 1985). Information on stamp-collecting came from the entry on "Philately" in the *Encyclopaedia Britannica* (Chicago, 1949). The literature on gardening is an old one and includes Francis Bacon's *Of gardens* (London, undated), Horace Walpole's *Essay on Modern Gardening* (Canton, Pa., 1904), and W. Carew Hazlitt's *Gleanings in Old Garden Literature* (London, 1887). I also consulted Danielle Régnier-Bohler's "Imagining the Self" in *A History of Private Life: Revelations of the Medieval World* (Georges Duby, ed., trans. Arthur Goldhammer, Cambridge, Mass., 1988), and Orest Ranum's "Refuges of Intimacy" in *A History of Private Life: Passions of the Renaissance* (Roger Chartier, ed., trans. Arthur Goldhammer, Cambridge, Mass., 1989). There are many histories of landscape architecture, including Edward Hyams's *A History of Gardens and Gardening* (New York, 1971), and *The Poetics of Gardens* (Cambridge, Mass., 1988), by Charles W. Moore, William J. Mitchell, and William Turnbull, Jr. On national gardening habits: Max Kaplan, *Leisure in America* (New York, 1960); K. Roberts, "Great Britain: Socioeconomic Polarization and the Implications for Leisure" in *Leisure and Lifestyle* (Anna Olszewska and K. Roberts, eds., London, 1989); Gyorgy Fukasz, "Hungary: More Work, Less Leisure" (also in *Leisure and Lifestyle*); and on Australia, Ian P. B. Halkett, "The Recreational Use of Private Gardens" (*Journal of Leisure Research*, 10, 1, 1978). I mention Johan H. Huizinga's *Homo Ludens: A Study of the Play-Element in Culture* (Boston, 1955) here but it was a book that influenced me throughout.

Anthony Storr's engaging study is *Solitude: A Return to the Self* (New York, 1988).

9: The Problem of Leisure

Sándor Ferenczi's essay on the Sunday neurosis is contained in his *Further Contributions to the Theory and Technique of Psycho-Analysis* (trans. Jane Isabel Suttie, New York, 1952). Lippmann's article appeared in *Woman's Home Companion* (57, April 1930). Two books of many on leisure that were published in the thirties are: H. A. Overstreet's *A Guide to Civilized Loafing* (New York, 1934) and Arthur Newton Pack's *The Challenge of Leisure* (New York, 1934). Statistics on the recent increase in the length of the work week and the decrease in leisure time are from Peter T. Kilborn's "Tales from the Digital Treadmill" (*New York Times,* June 3, 1990) and Jerome Richard's "Out of Time" (*New York Times,* Nov. 28, 1988). The University of Maryland and Michigan surveys are cited by Louis S. Richman in "Why the Middle Class is Anxious," *Fortune* (May 21, 1990). The theory of a shift to goods-intensive leisure was put forward by Staffan B. Linder in *The Harried Leisure Class* (New York, 1970). Arlie Hochschild's penetrating study *The Second Shift: Working Parents and the Revolution at*

Home (New York, 1989) is indirectly referred to. Bertrand Russell's "In Praise of Idleness" is only partly tongue-in-cheek; it is contained in *In Praise of Idleness and Other Essays* (London, 1935). The idea of sacred and profane time was proposed by Mircea Eliade in his classic *The Sacred and the Profane* (trans. Willard R. Trask, New York, 1959); descriptions of Navajo hogans are from Peter Nabokov and Robert Easton's exemplary study, *Native American Architecture* (New York, 1989). The suggestion that the weekend might be linked to sacred time is made by Anthony Aveni in *Empires of Time: Calendars, Clocks, and Cultures* (New York, 1989). On European leisure habits: Anthony Edwards, *Leisure Spending in The European Community: Forecasts to 1990* (London, 1981); and on the difference between Canada and the United States, Seymour Martin Lipset's *Continental Divide: The Values and Institutions of the United States and Canada* (New York, 1990). Finally, I am indebted to my friend John Lukacs for the insightful suggestion that the worlds of work and leisure may have come to represent two cultures. Indeed, they have.

Index

251

Index

Index

Index